WALKING THE CUMBRIA WAY

WALKING THE CUMBRIA WAY

ULVERSTON TO CARLISLE – MAIN ROUTE WITH MOUNTAIN ALTERNATIVES

by John Gillham

JUNIPER HOUSE, MURLEY MOSS,
OXENHOLME ROAD, KENDAL, CUMBRIA LA9 7RL
www.cicerone.co.uk

© John Gillham 2022
Second edition 2022
ISBN: 978 1 78631 133 7
Reprinted 2024 (with updates)
First edition 2015
Printed by Bell & Bain, Glasgow, on responsibly sourced paper
and other controlled sources.
All photographs are by the author unless otherwise stated.

This product includes mapping data licensed from Ordnance Survey® with the permission of the Controller of Her Majesty's Stationery Office.
© Crown copyright and database rights 2022 OS AC0000810376

Acknowledgements

I would like to thank my wife Nicola for being a constant companion, my good friend Ronald Turnbull for sharing his knowledge of geology, all the fine innkeepers of Cumbria, who kept Nicola and I fed and watered throughout our journeys and Paddy Dillon for showing me around his home town Ulverston and sparking my interest in the Cumbria Way.

Updates to this Guide

While every effort is made by our authors to ensure the accuracy of guidebooks as they go to print, changes can occur during the lifetime of an edition. Any updates that we know of for this guide will be on the Cicerone website (www.cicerone.co.uk/1133/updates), so please check before planning your trip. We also advise that you check information about such things as transport, accommodation and shops locally. Even rights of way can be altered over time. We are always grateful for information about any discrepancies between a guidebook and the facts on the ground, sent by email to updates@cicerone.co.uk.

Register your book: To sign up to receive free updates, special offers and GPX files where available, create a Cicerone account and register your purchase via the 'My Account' tab at www.cicerone.co.uk.

Front cover: In Great Langdale above Oakdale Farm (Stage 3)

CONTENTS

Map key 7

INTRODUCTION 9
The Cumbria Way. 10
The mountain way 12
Wildlife and plants 13
Geology (Ronald Turnbull) 16
When to go 18
Getting there 19
Accommodation. 20
Safety 22
Planning your itinerary 22
What to take. 24
Maps 26
Using GPS 26
Using this guide 28

THE CUMBRIA WAY 29
Stage 1   Ulverston to Coniston (or Torver). 30
Stage 2   Coniston (or Torver) to Great Langdale 44
Stage 2A   Torver to Great Langdale – mountain route 55
Stage 3   Great Langdale to Keswick 61
Stage 3A   Great Langdale to Keswick – mountain route 74
Stage 4   Keswick to Caldbeck. 85
Stage 4A   Keswick to Caldbeck – mountain route 95
Stage 4B   Keswick to Caldbeck – foul weather route. 100
Stage 5   Caldbeck to Carlisle 106

Appendix A   Route summary table 119
Appendix B   Facilities table. 121
Appendix C   Accommodation stage by stage 125
Appendix D   Useful contacts. 128

The 'foul weather route' down from Dash Falls (Stage 4)

MAP KEY

Route symbols on OS map extracts
(for OS legend see printed OS maps)

- ～ route
- ～ alternative route
- Ⓚ start point
- Ⓚ finish point
- Ⓢ alternative start
- Ⓕ alternative finish
- ◄ route direction

Features on the overview map

- ——— County/Unitary boundary
- ——— National boundary
- Urban area
- National Park
- Area of Outstanding Natural Beauty

200m	800m
75m	600m
0m	400m

GPX files
for all routes can be downloaded free at www.cicerone.co.uk/1133/GPX

The leafy beauty of Borrowdale seen here at Gowder Dub near Castle Crag (Stage 3)

Last look at the Lakes from the path beneath Lonscale Fell (Stage 4)

INTRODUCTION

Skiddaw and Keswick from Walla Crag's summit (Stage 3A)

Cumbria sits pretty at the north-western edge of England. Its beauty is timeless, one that inspired Wordsworth and the other Lakeland Romantic poets – Coleridge, Ruskin, Keats and Shelley – to stay and write in this place of lakes, riverside woodland and high fell. If you're looking for a place to walk, where better than here? And if you're looking for a long-distance walk that you can do in a week, look no further than the Cumbria Way.

At just over 73 miles (117km) long the Cumbria Way allows you time to walk but also time to look around and be inspired by these great landscapes too. It takes in all that is best in the Lake District – views of the majestic fells, lakeshore promenades and strolls through woodland, past waterfalls, picturesque cottages and fine inns. Devised by local Ramblers' Association groups during the 1970s, the route starts in Ulverston, not far from the shores of Morecambe Bay, and finishes in the city of Carlisle.

The official route is largely a low-level walk though the valleys of Cumbria and suitable for any experienced walkers. The mountain route included here in not an official variant but offers a more challenging, high-level alternative for those who prefer the summits to the valleys and the passes. Both are ideal for campers and youth hostellers as much as those preferring a bit of comfort or even luxury on their holidays. The latter group can ease through leafy Cumbria in style and dine in some of the country pubs for which the Lake District is famous but there are also plenty of good campsites and youth hostels throughout the journey.

THE CUMBRIA WAY

The walk out of Ulverston starts well, on a little beckside path, and more often than not the continuing route is pretty. However there are lots of field paths to negotiate and it's hard to get up any momentum. By the time you get to Gawthwaite you'll feel you won't make it to Coniston – but you will. The second half of the day seems to go more quickly than the first and the paths get easier to follow and you will be drawn on by glimpses of the Coniston Fells peeping above low hills and moors on the horizon.

The Lake District proper starts small, with Beacon Tarn, a lake in miniature, surrounded by small but rocky and perfectly-formed hills. And those Coniston Fells get nearer and nearer, their rock faces more and more defined. Towards the end of the day you're strolling on easy paths by Coniston Water, staring across at Ruskin's Brantwood home and contemplating Wordsworth's daffodils. (If you're a month or two too late you can buy the postcard!)

The next day the Cumbria Way goes into the heart of the Lake District, taking in more tarns, waterfalls in the woods and whitewashed

It all begins here at Ulverston's Cumbria Way sculpture

Tarn Hows (Stage 2)

cottages with rose gardens. It enters Great Langdale, where the rocks form great buttresses and gullies and the mountains become distinctive and tantalising temples. Beneath them sits the Old Dungeon Ghyll Hotel – a fine place to stop, eat and discuss tomorrow's route with fellow travellers.

You look to the skies for the next day's route and there's no obvious way out. The route goes over the 500m Stake Pass. It's steep but short-lived and the path is easy to follow. Next you tackle the lovely Langstrath, a wild, uninhabited valley with nothing but a bouldery river and bouldery mountainsides for comfort. It's a long way to Keswick from Langdale, maybe too long, so when you see the beautiful, ever-so-green and lush Borrowdale you may feel the urge to make this an overnight stop.

Rosthwaite and Grange are pleasantly peaceful places in the middle of these beautiful mountain and riverscapes.

Derwent Water is a prince among the Lake District lakes and that view of Skiddaw's smooth pastel pink and green-shaded slopes is exquisite. Keswick at its north end is lively, a place to restock, maybe recover, before the long day over the Back o' Skidda to Caldbeck. Those who stopped at Rosthwaite are lucky as long as they've pre-booked the hostel at Skiddaw House. They will find they've discovered one of the most remote and romantic locations en route and they will have shortened the next day to Caldbeck.

As long as you're confident enough about the weather to ignore the inferior foul weather Bassenthwaite route, the day out of

Rosthwaite in Borrowdale (Stage 3)

Keswick will be highlighted by reaching the summit of High Pike, highest place on the whole of the official Cumbria Way at over 2000 feet. It's an airy place with an orientation table to show you the hundreds of hills in view, including the Scottish ones across the Solway Firth.

Looking north you can see that there are no more big hills left in England. Between you and your destination there are low ridges and mile upon mile of pastureland. The last day will be remembered for its riverside scenery. The Caldew, which you first saw near Skiddaw House, will guide you all the way, including through the streets of Carlisle, where the cathedral quarter is rich in the histories of both England and Scotland. It's a fitting end to a truly memorable walk.

THE MOUNTAIN WAY

If all this is not exciting enough, why not add in some mountains? The mountain variants described come down to meet the official route at convenient points, allowing you to mix and match according to the weather and your inclination or mood, and if followed in total only add about 3 miles (5km) to the overall distance. The official Cumbria Way passes beneath the Coniston range but by leaving it at Torver the mountain route takes in Goat's Water, Swirl How and Great Carrs. It then descends to Slater's Bridge, one of the prettiest ancient packhorse bridges in Cumbria, before rejoining the 'Way' at Elterwater on the edge of Great Langdale.

The moraine scenery of Stake Pass above Great Langdale is fascinating but climbing beneath the buttresses

The wild beauty of the Back o' Skidda with Skiddaw House sheltering among the larch trees (Stage 4)

of Bowfell, past Angle Tarn and onto the high peaks of Allen Crags and Glaramara is more spectacular. The views of Borrowdale that open up on the descent from Thornythwaite Fell make the day worthwhile on their own. Walla Crag comes next. It's not big but it's got a well-sculpted rock and heather top with superb views of Derwent Water, Bassenthwaite Lake and the surrounding fells.

The big one is Skiddaw, one of the Lake District's 3000 footers. If the day is a fine one Skiddaw is so close that you've got to do it. If the day is too big you can drop down from the summit to the hostel at Skiddaw House. Either way, Great Calva, Knott and High Pike can be included in a high-level traverse to Caldbeck.

Cumbria runs out of mountains beyond Caldbeck so the now-hardened mountain walker can take it easy and follow the official route by the Caldew into Carlisle, knowing that they have completed the 'Cumbria Mountain Way'.

WILDLIFE AND PLANTS

Once much of Cumbria would have been covered by oak woodland but today's mosaic of diverse landscapes has been shaped by widespread farming and grazing by deer and sheep. Sheep and cow pastures form a large part of the early Cumbria Way landscape between Ulverston and Gawthwaite and although you'll see some wildflowers the continuous grazing means species are limited. The thin acid soils of the Coniston foothills mean that bracken, rushes and cotton grass proliferate with the odd birch

Above Stable Harvey Moss (Stage 1)

tree and juniper bushes scattered across the fellsides. In the marshy areas by Beacon Tarn you'll also see bog myrtle, a deciduous shrub about a metre tall with oval leaves. Its oils are claimed to repel biting insects.

Although adders are quite common in the dry moors and mountains of the Lake District you'll probably not see any on this route. If you are lucky enough to see one basking on a rock, leave it be for it will almost certainly slither away into the undergrowth when it spots you.

As the path makes its way through mountain valleys there will be ravens and buzzards soaring on thermals around the crags above, searching for carrion. The sheep are still here in the low fell country so the main colour will be provided by the larger 'less tasty' flowers like the bright yellow gorse and the purple-pink foxgloves. Primroses, bluebells, wood anemone, wood sorrel, herb robert and red campion will be confined to woodland and hedgerow.

Many of the modern forests are made up of spruce, pine and larch, although the old coppiced woodland still covers the central regions of the park, especially so between Coniston and Langdale and in Borrowdale. The high rainfall in the sessile oakwoods of Borrowdale has helped propagate lichens, liverworts and insects, which in turn have offered a habitat for various owls, peregrine falcons, pied flycatchers and greater spotted woodpeckers. In the rivers and streams there are otters and you may well see the dipper, a small active

The Yewdale Fells and a waterfall from Back Guards Plantation above Coniston (Stage 2)

dark brown white-chested bird that bobs and dives into the waters looking for insects. I've seen grey herons on the River Derwent near Grange. These large long-necked wading birds wait, ever so still and patient, for an unsuspecting fish to pass by. They are mesmerising to watch.

Although it's in serious decline in southern Britain the shy red squirrel still thrives in the woods of central Cumbria. Elsewhere it has been displaced by the larger grey squirrel, which was introduced from North America.

As the Way approaches Derwent Water's flood plains you'll be able to see more bog myrtle, also alder woodland and reed beds, which are ideal for wildfowl and wading birds, including sandpipers. Beneath the waters of the lake is a rare fish, the vendace, which only exists in four British lakes.

In the 1990s ospreys were seen feeding in Bassenthwaite Lake. They had been absent from Cumbria for over 150 years and the Lake District Osprey Project was set up to encourage them to nest here. A nesting platform was erected in woodland above the lake. In 2001 the project's efforts bore fruit and a chick successfully fledged, the first of many. If you have any time to spare there are viewing platforms in Dodds Wood off the A591 west of Keswick.

The Skiddaw and Back a' Skidda peaks have thin soils and very few plant species other than expansive carpets of heather, a perfect habitat for the red grouse and the insect-eating sundew.

GEOLOGY

Contributed by Ronald Turnbull

You're clinging to a GPS satellite, looking down on the shoreline of a continent like the edge of South America today. Along the continental edge runs a great range of volcanoes, just like the Andes. Offshore is a deep ocean trench, slowly filling up with mud and sludge. And in behind the mountains on the landward side, a shallow, muddy-bottomed sea. Suddenly, another continent crashes in from the north: in another 400 million years we'll be calling it Scotland. Meanwhile, the crushed and crumpled remains of the ocean sludge, volcanoes, and muddy sea floor: these form the three sorts of Lakeland rocks. In the course of the Cumbria Way you'll walk across them all.

But before all that, something completely different. The Cumbria Way starts on a much younger rock, the Mountain (or Carboniferous) Limestone. This makes grand scenery in the Yorkshire Dales and the Mendips, but in southern Cumbria it has been worn down into a gentle landscape of fields and woods. See the pale, yellowish-brown limestone best in the houses and field walls of Ulverston.

As you enter the national park, you're walking onto the first of the true Lakeland rocks: the grey sea-bottom mudstones and sandstones of the Windermere Supergroup. They're younger than other Lakeland rocks

Great Carrs from Swirl How (Stage 2A)

(Silurian period) and also softer, so the scenery is still gentle and mountain-free. You'll see the slabby mudstones in outcrops north of Beacon Tarn. Around Coniston village, some of them form flat flagstones that are tilted on edge and used as field walls.

But where the Silurian stones most show is where they stop, as they give way to the tough, rugged Borrowdale Volcanics. The sudden start of the mountain ground is obvious as you approach Coniston Old Man. These rocks mostly fell from the sky as volcanic ash, the stuff that much more recently smothered Pompeii. Valley rocks are mossy and weathered, but in clean mountain crags, on riverbeds, and in the foot-worn path, you can see the various different volcanic disasters. There's ash with sprinkled volcanic gravel (lapilli) or larger lumps of pumice. There's ash that fell into crater lakes, now delicately striped in shades of grey. There's chunky 'block tuff', which formed as landslides of ash and broken stone. Most striking of all when you see it, there's 'ignimbrite'. This was a red-hot flying avalanche of ash, gas and pumice; one such at St Pierre in Martinique travelled down the mountainside at 60mph and killed 35,000 townspeople in the space of a few seconds. Once at rest and as it all welds together, the hot pumice bits flatten to pale elongated streaks.

North of Keswick, the mountains change. The line is actually crossed on the way up Borrowdale: look at the left-hand valley wall above Hollows Farm. The Skiddaw Slates, originally ocean-bottom sludge, form few

High in valley of Glenderaterra Beck (Stage 4)

spectacular crags, instead creating tall, steep slopes of heather over scree, and elegant ridgelines along the top.

The northern edge of Lakeland is as sudden as the south was; and you're back on the Mountain Limestone. Admire the limestone gorge called the Howk, at the edge of Caldbeck. On the Cumbria Way path itself, you might spot a stream emerging in the Caldew's bank out of an authentic limestone cavern.

And you finish on a fifth, quite different, sort of stone. The desert dunes of the New Red Sandstone show in the Caldew banks, but best of all where they rise in the pink 'cliffs' of Carlisle's castle and cathedral.

WHEN TO GO

April and May are best for wildflowers and vivid colours – the bracken is still red and contrasts beautifully with the fresh green leaves of the forests. The days are still short but, if you're a photographer, the sun creates a much better light with pleasing shadows to give depth to your pictures. Also, the campsites and B&Bs won't be at full capacity and will be more reasonably priced.

Summer is obviously warmer, meaning you'll need less clothing in your rucksack, and the long days give you more time to get to your destination. There would be more time to see the attractions on the way (if you keep a careful eye on closing times).

Autumn is still good, with the woods, and there are lots of them on the route, displaying beautiful fiery colours. Often the British weather is quite settled at this time.

Winter days are short so you'd need to break down the route into more sections and you'd need to pack far more clothes and equipment. Snow and ice would add to the difficulties, especially on the crossing of Stake Pass between Langdale and Borrowdale and the traverse over the Back o' Skidda. Most of the campsites, youth hostels and small B&Bs will be closed at this time.

GETTING THERE

By train

The Cumbria Coastal Line linking Lancaster and Carlisle via Barrow and the Cumbria coast calls at Ulverston. It is operated by Trans Pennine and Northern Rail. Both Carlisle and

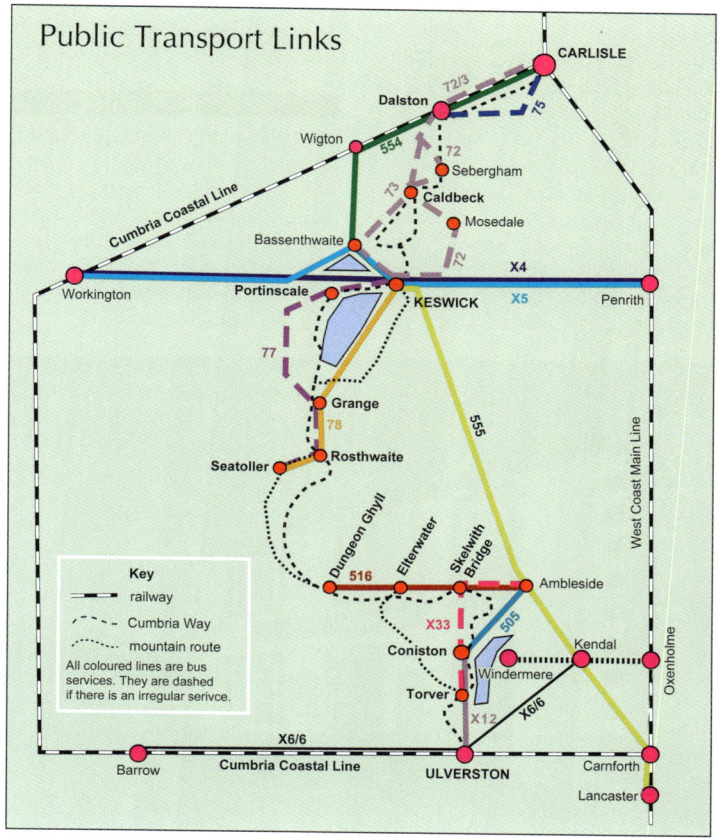

Lancaster are on the West Coast Main Line linking Glasgow and London Euston. Carlisle also has a rail link to Newcastle-upon-Tyne and Dalston (near the end of the walk) is on the Cumbria Coastal Line with links to both Ulverston and Carlisle. For more information: www.thetrainline.com.

By bus
The regular X6 service, run by Stagecoach, between Kendal and Barrow, stops at Ulverston. The No 6 links Ulverston with the railway station at Windermere, linked to West Coast line via Oxenholme. For the latest information on buses see www.cumbria.gov.uk. Select 'find a bus timetable' from the 'roads and travel' drop down menu. For long distance coaches to and from Carlisle or Kendal (the nearest coach stop for Ulverston) visit www.nationalexpress.com.

Between stages
In case you wish to walk a stage as a day walk or if you need to skip a day or get home urgently, public transport links between stages are described in detail in Appendix D.

ACCOMMODATION

The range of accommodation available in the Lake District is wide. Most stage starts and finishes on this route, being sizeable tourist destinations, will be no exception to this rule. Even in Great Langdale there are three pubs, a handful of places offering B&B and some campsites.

Getting ready for a new day after a night in the Oddfellows Arms, Caldbeck (Stage 5)

Eagle Crag from near Smithymire Island (Stage 3)

Accommodation providers are always changing and so it would be impractical to try and provide a complete listing here. The table in Appendix B gives an indication of the accommodation available along the route. A selection of the larger pubs and B&Bs is also listed, stage by stage, in Appendix C, along with a more comprehensive list of hostels and campsites, which tend to be less transient, and some useful websites for finding up-to-date information are also listed in Appendix D.

SAFETY

It is extremely important that you are fully equipped and practised in the use of map and compass. Your well-being may depend on it. While the Cumbria Way spends most of its time in the valleys and low hills it does climb to the Stake Pass and High Pike, two remote spots where help is not immediately at hand.

Make sure to take enough food and water and keep additional emergency rations in the corner of the rucksack. Not taking enough food is the quickest way of becoming tired, and being tired is the quickest way of sustaining an injury.

Good breathable waterproofs are essential. Remember, getting cold and wet will make you vulnerable to hypothermia, even outside the winter months. It is important to wear good walking boots. Shoes and trainers have insufficient grip and ankle support on difficult terrain and even the lower-level sections can become slippery after rainfall. It is a good idea to pack some emergency medical supplies (such as plasters and bandages): there are plenty of good first aid kits available.

The mountain routes have been designed to mix and match with the official route and will spend no more than a day away from it. They are all safe for experienced walkers in clement conditions, but in wintry conditions become more challenging and hazardous. If these conditions were likely, it would be better to divert to the official way. If you do decide to go for the mountains in wintry conditions, let somebody know of your plans and take an ice axe and crampons. It's also essential that you know how to use them. Be ready to turn around where necessary and always be prepared to adjust your itinerary.

PLANNING YOUR ITINERARY

This guide follows tradition and describes the Cumbria Way from south to north – Ulverston to Carlisle. If you walk the route this way, in the same direction as the prevailing UK weather, you should have the sun and the wind on your back. Also, Carlisle's cathedral quarter offers a grand finale to your adventure.

The route description is divided into five stages. Each one could be completed in a day but everybody has their own pace. A route summary

PLANNING YOUR ITINERARY

ALTERNATIVE SCHEDULES

Easy	Distance
Day 1 Ulverston to Cockenskell Farm (B&B)	9½ miles (14.5km)
Day 2 Cockenskell Farm to Coniston	6 miles (9.5km)
Day 3 Coniston to Elterwater	8¼ miles (13km)
Day 4 Elterwater to Rosthwaite	11¼ miles (19km)
Day 5 Rosthwaite to Keswick	8¼ miles (13km)
Day 6 Keswick to Skiddaw House	5½ miles (9km)
Day 7 Skiddaw House to Caldbeck	9 miles (14.5km)
Day 8 Caldbeck to Dalston	9¾ miles* (15.5km)
Day 9 Dalston to Carlisle	5¾ miles (9km)

* If you stop at Dalston there is a campsite or upmarket hotel at Dalston Hall. Alternatively you could catch a bus or train to Carlisle and return to Dalston the next morning.

Moderate	Distance
Day 1 Ulverston to Torver	12 miles (19km)
Day 2 Torver to Elterwater	11¾ miles (19km)
Day 3 Elterwater to Rosthwaite	11¼ miles (18km)
Day 4 Rosthwaite to Skiddaw House	13¾ miles (22km)
Day 5 Skiddaw House to Caldbeck	9 miles (14.5km)
Day 6 Caldbeck to Carlisle	15½ miles (25km)

Mountain Route	Distance
Day 1 Ulverston to Torver	12 miles (19km)
Day 2 Torver to Elterwater	12 miles (19km)
Day 3 Elterwater to Lodore	16 miles (25.5km)
Day 4 Lodore to Skiddaw House	13 miles* (21km)
Day 5 Skiddaw House to Caldbeck	8 miles (13km)
Day 6 Caldbeck to Carlisle	15½ miles (25km)

* Day 4 could be shortened by stopping the night at Keswick. This would make it a 7-day itinerary.

of the main route is provided in Appendix A and some alternative itineraries are offered here to help you plan your own trip.

WHAT TO TAKE

What you take depends on how you're going to tackle the route. If you're camping you'll need additional gear: a tent, sleeping bags, a sleeping mat/Thermarest, cooking stove and utensils. If you're hostelling you'll need a sleeping bag. If you're using a baggage transfer company or being taken along the route by a guiding company (see Appendix D), you will need a day sack but you will not need to worry as much about the total weight you are taking with you.

The basics
- good rucksack: 35 litre or more for B&B-ing; 45 litre or more for youth hostelling; 55 litre or more for camping.
- liner or plastic carrier bags to keep your gear dry inside the rucksack
- breathable waterproofs both jackets and trousers
- good proven waterproof boots
- walking socks
- fleece jacket or warm sweater
- warm hat and gloves
- changes of clothes for evening wear
- sun hat and sun cream (outside winter months)
- first aid kit (including plasters for blisters)

At Lever's Hawse with Coniston Old Man Brim Fell and Dow Crag behind (Stage 2A)

Grains Gill, Back o' Skidda (Stage 4)

- whistle and torch in case of emergencies
- mobile phone (but be aware that there are many 'no reception' areas in Cumbria.
- food and plenty of fluids for the day
- tissues (in case you get caught short)
- compass, maps and guidebook

Optional
- a GPS unit or GPS app and maps for your smartphone. These days GPS units are excellent companions, whether they be 7" tablets or specialist units like Garmin or Memory Map (see Using GPS, below).

MAPS

The map extracts in this guide are from OS Landranger® maps (1:50,000). You should also take the following 1:25,000 Explorer® maps for greater detail:
- OL6 (Ulverston to Coniston)
- OL7 (Coniston to Great Langdale)
- OL4 (Great Langdale to Skiddaw House)
- OL5 (Skiddaw House to Dalston)
- 315 (Dalston to Carlisle)

Harvey Maps publish a dedicated Cumbria Way 1:40,000 map, which is convenient because everything is on one water-resistant map and it also includes useful town plans. Unfortunately it is harder to follow the routes on the ground as field boundaries are not marked and everything is a bit small. In addition to this, some of this book's mountain routes would be off this Harvey map.

USING GPS

In recent years global positioning system (GPS) units such as those made by Garmin, Memory Map and Satmap have become quite sophisticated and now they usually include OS mapping for the UK. They are a very useful addition to your equipment, especially if you're caught out in hill fog on the mountains.

In addition to the dedicated GPS units there are aps for iPhones, Android and Blackberry smartphones and tablets too. Viewranger and Memory Map are the best known and their maps, which are stored on your phone rather being online 'in the cloud' (like Trailzilla maps). Remember, if the maps are in the cloud and you don't have a phone signal, then you don't have a map, so download everything you need before leaving.

Map packages
Most dedicated units come with map packages. Some come with complete OS Landranger 1:50,000 maps for the UK, while others just include national parks. Be warned that the first section from Ulverston to Gawthwaite and the last section north of Caldbeck to Carlisle are not within the National Park boundary. OS Explorer maps are

better and you can buy DVDs for the whole of the UK although they are expensive. The other way of doing this is by going online and downloading the exact area you want (Memory Map and Viewranger both enable this to be done). You can always add to the area you bought later.

Charging the units

All units will need charging at the end of the day. Dedicated GPS units can usually last eight hours and most do have facilities to attach battery cases to keep them topped up.

The batteries in smartphones are smaller and won't last all day when used as a GPS – probably about 2–4 hours. You may need at least one spare battery or you'll have to use it sparingly, that is, when you're unsure of where to go next. Tablets such as the iPad Mini and Android 7-inch ones usually have larger batteries and can be kept in waterproof cases, which can hang around your neck, in the same way as map cases do. Aquapac do a fine range of such cases. The tablets have the advantage of showing you large areas of the map at once.

If you cannot get to a power source to recharge your unit you can buy portable chargers. I bought a 12000mAh EasyAcc one that will recharge an iPhone six or seven times or an iPad Mini twice before it needs recharging itself. (mAh stands for milli Ampere hour, a measure of a battery's energy storage capacity – the

Looking across the Back o' Skidda from the summit of High Pike (Stage 4)

On the summit of Knott (Stage 4A)

higher the mAh figure the better.) A 6000mAh, for instance, would only charge the iPhone three times.

A word of caution here: these units should be used as a supplement to the maps – batteries may lose power unexpectedly.

USING THIS GUIDE

Each stage of route description in this guide is illustrated on extracts from the 1:50,000 OS Landranger maps. Features highlighted in bold in the step-by-step route description should be those that appear on these map extracts. Simplified street maps are also included for Ulverston, Keswick and Carlisle. They should make it much easier to navigate your way through the towns.

Free GPX tracks for the official route and the mountain alternatives can also be downloaded by anyone who has bought this guide by visiting www.cicerone.co.uk/1133/gpx.

An indication of the distance, terrain, ascent and a rough time to allow are given at the start of each stage along with a list of the recommended OS maps and anywhere to stock up on supplies en route. Information about things to do at the stage ends and starts is also provided in separate boxes for walkers who find themselves with time in hand or the need to fill a rest day.

THE CUMBRIA WAY

Descending from the col above Beacon Tarn (Stage 1)

STAGE 1
Ulverston to Coniston (or Torver)

Start	The Gill, Ulverston
Distance	15½ miles (25km); 12 miles (19km) to Torver
Ascent	615m
Approx time	7–8 hours; 6–7 hours to Torver
Terrain	farmland, country lane, low fell and level lakeside path
Map	OS Explorer OL6 South Western area
Supplies	no cafés, shops or pubs before Torver which does have one shop with general supplies

It's all too easy to dwell too long exploring Ulverston's cobbled streets or watching the world go by in one of its cosy cafés but if you intend to walk to Coniston you need to be off by 11am at the latest. The tree-lined stream out of town makes a pleasant start but the early part of the route is bitty, across pastures that can be muddy after rain and through farmyards and along country lanes.

By the time you come to Gawthwaite you think you're not going to make it, but the navigation soon gets simpler. Views of the Coniston Fells become more frequent and more spectacular, the craggy Blawith Fells get closer and closer, and before you know it you're walking beside the idyllic Beacon Tarn. And the day (if it ends in Coniston) ends in a glorious promenade by the peaceful shores of Coniston Water. You may even be early enough for a boat trip on the Gondola.

The Way begins at the Cumbria Way monument in a square known as **The Gill**. In the north-west corner, marked by a blue 'start of the Cumbria Way' plaque a tarred path continues by a small stream. Turn left over a footbridge to cross the stream. On reaching a lane double back right on the nearside of that lane, following the direction set by a Cumbria Way fingerpost across fields, eventually to join a farm track to **Old Hall Farm**.

After turning right and passing through the farmyard and the farmhouse but just before a newer house, turn left through a gap stile in a wall – a fingerpost marks the

Stage 1 – Ulverston to Coniston (or Torver)

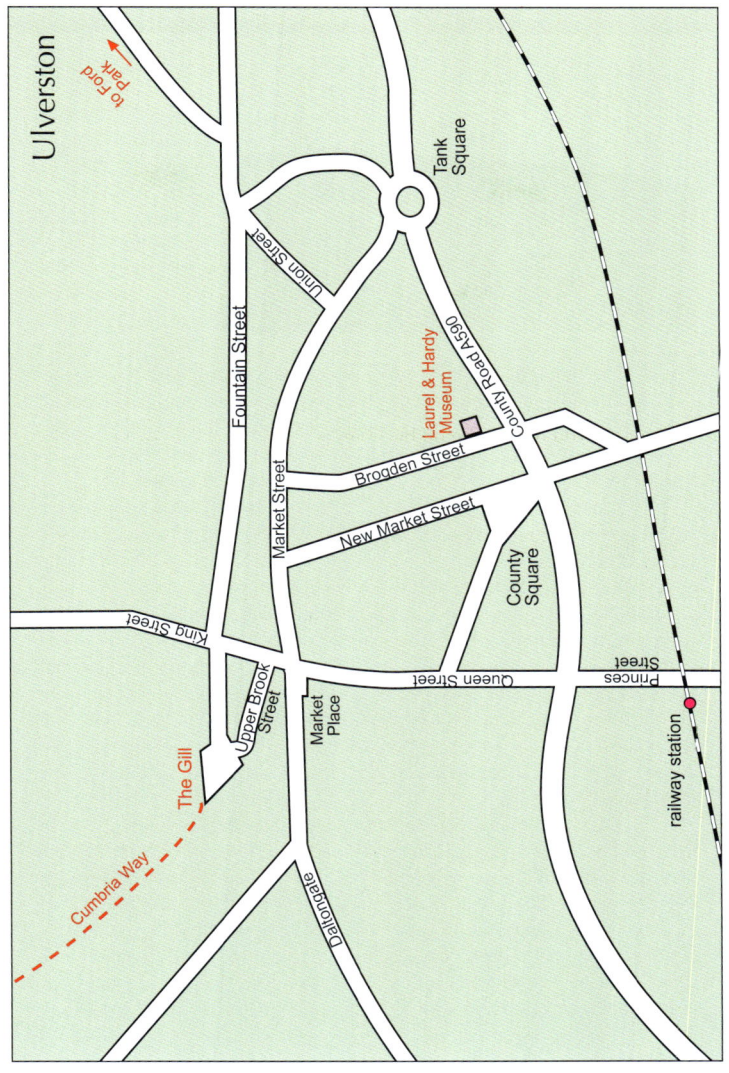

ULVERSTON

The Sir John Barrow Monument atop Hoad Hill

Ulverston is a busy but attractive market town sited on coastal pastureland bordering the wide Leven Estuary. It is sheltered to the north by low grassy hills and connected to the sea by the 1¼-mile Ulverston Canal. Completed in 1796 the canal opened up maritime trade in timber, coal, iron, copper and gunpowder. Ships were built here and passenger ferries linked the now prosperous town with Liverpool. Unfortunately the coming of the Furness Railway in 1846 brought about the slow decline of the canal and by the end of the Second World War it ceased to operate.

The town is first recorded in the Domesday Book of 1086 as Ulureston, which comes from the words *Úlfarr* (a Norse name meaning wolf warrior) and *tūn* (a settlement – town or village), and it was granted its market charter by Edward I in 1280. The market is still held on Thursdays and Saturdays.

Looking up to the town's skyline, Hoad Hill's summit is topped by a white tower that looks remarkably like a lighthouse. Built in 1850 to commemorate Sir John Barrow, who in 1804 became the Admiralty's Second Secretary, it was indeed modelled on the third Eddystone Lighthouse (viewing platform open: Sundays and Bank Holiday Mondays 1pm–5pm, from Easter to the end of October, when the flag on the hill is flying; Ford Park at the foot of the hill has an excellent café and bistro with outdoor seating, http://ford-park.org.uk).

Ulverston has community spirit – you'll feel that when you arrive. It advertises itself as a 'Festival Town' and you may well be lucky enough to come here when one of the many is being held such as Ulverston WalkFest, the Dickensian Festival or one of the music festivals or Buddhist festivals. The community spent ten years raising £60,000 for bronze statues of film star comedians Stan Laurel and Oliver Hardy, which stand outside the Coronation Hall. Laurel, whose real name was Arthur Stanley Jefferson, was born in June 1890 in Argyle Street, Ulverston and, although he made his name in the US, he

Stage 1 – Ulverston to Coniston (or Torver)

The Laurel and Hardy statues

revisited the town with 'Ollie' in 1947 when the townsfolk gave them a tumultuous reception. (Laurel and Hardy Museum, Brogden Street, open: 10am–5pm Tues, Thurs, Fri, Sat, Sun, http://laurel-and-hardy-museum.co.uk)

If you walk along King Street from the Market Cross and turn right down the ginnel of Bolton's Place, also along Lower Brook Street on the other side of the Bodycare building you'll see the most amazing and colourful murals. Organised by the Clancy Youth Group and painted by Artist Gill Barron along with Ulverstonians young and old, the murals celebrate the town's 29 festivals and the life of Sir John Barrow. The hundreds of figures include St George, three dragons and a damsel in distress and illustrate the Pantomime Horse Race, egg rolling and the Lantern procession.

George Fox, founder of the Quaker movement, visited Ulverston many times to visit Judge Fell and his wife Margaret at nearby Swarthmoor Hall (Swarthmoor Hall, Swarthmoor Hall Lane, open Mon–Fri 10.30am–4.30pm, Sun 1.30pm–4.30pm, http://swarthmoorhall.co.uk).

Conishead Priory to the south east of the town is well worth a visit if you have time – you could even include it in the walk and use it as a coastal starting point. The 12th-century Augustinian Priory was founded in 1160 by Gamelde Pennington as a hospital for the 'poor, decrepit, indigent and lepers' of the Ulverston area. It became a priory 28 years later and then was dismantled following the Dissolution of the Monasteries. The current Gothic building dates back to 1821, built for Colonel Braddyll, whose family, resided here for two centuries. By the 1970s the building lay empty and decaying but in 1976 it became the home to the monks of the Manjushri Kadampa Meditation Centre who set about renovating the buildings and building a new temple based on traditional Buddhist architecture. Today, the priory, temple and wooded grounds are open to the public. (Conishead Priory, Conishead Priory Road (A5087 Coast Road) Ulverston, open Mon–Sat 11am–5pm, Sun 12–5pm; grounds from dawn to dusk, http://nkt-kmc-manjushri.org)

www.visitulverston.com

spot. Over another stile at the back of the farmhouse the route angles half right (NW) across fields, aiming for a stile at the right edge of woodland. Beyond the stile follow the woodland edge and go over another stile before climbing towards the large house of **Bortree Stile** on the hillside ahead. The path follows a streamlet and stays to the left of the house and its pleasant gardens, then goes through a gate into woodland. A narrow path continues by the streamlet then crosses it on a slab footbridge before entering high pastures.

> Looking to the right you'll see the rooftops of **Ulverston** beneath Hoad Hill and its monument, with the waters of Morecambe Bay and the distant hills of Bowland and Yorkshire Dales forming the backdrop.

Keep to the right of high ground and pass through a small hollow in the field to a stile on its far side. Beyond the stile the path continues through the hollow, but now among rock-strewn, gorse-scattered pastures. Over a step stile in a cross-wall the path crosses a field towards the farmhouse of **Higher Lath**, where it meets a country lane.

map continues on page 36

Here the Cumbria Way has been modified avoiding the section through Newbiggin. Turn right along the lane for about 170m (557ft). The new path turns left through a crudely signed farm gate before heading north on a furrowed track across a field. Go through the right of two gates and continue north to pass through another gateway. Beyond this angle right across the third field, go through a gate at the bottom, then follow a grass ramp before angling right to a wall corner by a wooden electricity pylon. Descend a few metres to a line of trees to meet the original route by a stile and stream crossing at SD 278 808. A waymarker arrow highlight the route NNW towards the left side of the **Stony Crag** Farm complex.

Behind the farmhouse angle right, away from a farm track, through a gate and follow the wall on the right before turning right through a waymarked gate and continuing with the field boundary to the left.

On nearing **Hollowmire** farm a Cumbria Way sign guides the way on a short enclosed grass path leading to the farmhouse. Turn right through the farmyard and follow the farm lane out to the road, where you should turn left.

A wooden signpost at a left hand bend points the way right through a farm gate, beyond which a faint path leads across more fields to the 19th-century slate and sandstone **church** of St John the Evangelist. An enclosed

St John's Church near Broughton Beck

WALKING THE CUMBRIA WAY

map continues on page 38

track to the left of the church leads to the road, where you turn right. Turn left at a T-junction, then right along the lane leading to the village of **Broughton Beck**.

Where the road veers right in the heart of the village, turn left on a cul-de-sac. The lane bends left then the tarmac ends. Continue along a track, soon coming to the stream (Broughton Beck). One path fords the stream, but the one you want goes straight ahead through a metal farm gate. The way continues past large outbuildings and through a long field before veering right at a signpost and passing through a wall step stile into the next field. Angle half left to locate a slabbed slate bridge across the beck near the left edge of the field. Turn left by the stream's banks and go over a stile. The route now follows the left-hand field boundaries (walls and hedges) across several fields to join a rough track, which climbs to an unfenced lane beneath a rugged low hill, Lowick Beacon (**211m spot height** on the map).

Turn left along the lane, passing **Knapperthaw** farm. Take the right fork lane at the far end of the farm, then fork left on a shortcut track by the next junction. Now take the track opposite, which takes the route towards **Keldray** farm.

By now the mountains of **Dow Crag**, **Coniston Old Man** and **Wetherlam** can be seen clearly above the nearby woods and hillside and the Lake District proper feels a little nearer.

Beyond a gate before the house turn left – the place is marked by a ground-level signpost pointing up wooded slopes.

STAGE 1 – ULVERSTON TO CONISTON (OR TORVER)

Ignore the first stile on the left but climb steps to cross the stile above. Beyond this turn right along the upper edge of the woods and then the farmhouse. After another stile veer slightly left up the sloping field to a gate in the middle of the far wall – if you follow the line of wooden pylons you'll see this gate a few metres to the left. Follow the top wall of the next field.

Over a stile the route follows a path enclosed by walls. This leads to the first houses of **Gawthwaite**. Follow a tarred lane past more houses to reach the busy **A5092**. ▶

Cross the road before taking a minor tarred lane staggered very slightly to the left between the houses. Take the right fork, then the left beyond the last house onto a walled lane signed 'public way to Gawthwaite Land'. This climbs past quarries and high pastures, with the valley of the **River Crake** and the little wooded hills beyond leading the eyes to their first glimpse of Coniston Water.

After about two thirds of a mile along the lane and just beyond a gate by a long narrow stand of trees, take the right fork track descending high pastures before winding around three sides of **High Stennerley**. The track becomes a tarred lane beneath the attractive gardens of the farmhouse and descends further to a country lane at **Kendall Ground**.

Turn right along the lane for 30m before turning left to follow the direction set by a wooden fingerpost and tractor wheel-tracks. Where the track divides take the right fork, which keeps higher ground to the left. The narrow path comes to a gate with an adjacent step stile then fades, but go right alongside an overgrown hedge – noting a waymarking arrow on a boulder.

Keep the rushy ground to your right and ignore a tall wooden post, which would have you fighting a way through thickets. ▶ Beyond this the path maintains direction, following a derelict, grassed-over wall to the right. This leads to a stile in a drystone wall (only visible at the last moment of the slight descent). Beyond the stile descend a few paces to a country lane, where you should turn left.

Now the route has entered the Lake District National Park, although it will still be traversing pastureland rather than mountainside for a while yet.

It will hopefully rot away and confuse no more.

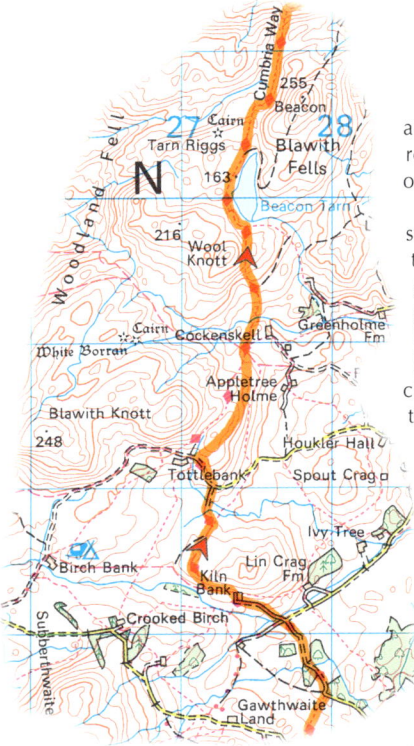

The lane winds through trees and among pastureland scattered with rocks and soon nears a landscape overlooked by low craggy hills.

Where the lane turns right go straight on along a tarred farm road to **Kiln Bank**. Turn right through a gate just past the farm and follow a grass track, which, beyond the buildings, veers left to follow a wall on the left. Take the signed right fork track climbing open hillside. On reaching the top of the hill it fades but boot marks and tyre tracks are still visible as they thread their way between scattered thorn trees.

There's a slight bend to the right before coming to a gate and ladder stile in a cross-wall. Beyond this a clear track arcs left, eventually to meet a high country lane. Turn left along the lane with the whitewashed **Tottlebank** farm in the distance backed up by the even craggier Blawith Fells.

Approaching Beacon Tarn in the Blawith Fells

STAGE 1 – ULVERSTON TO CONISTON (OR TORVER)

Just before the farm leave the lane for a signed grass track on the right climbing hillsides patched with bracken. ▶ After scaling the shoulder of Tottlebank Fell it descends towards **Cockenskell** farm and joins a track coming in from the right. Just beyond this go through a gate on the right and follow the wall on the left across a field, keeping the farm well to the right.

This begins at SD 271 882 and is not the route as shown on current OS maps.

At the far end of the field follow an enclosed grass track with trees to the right. Go through a gate and descend to cross a stream on a little footbridge before climbing the far banks. The route will now climb to the highlights of the day – the Blawith Fells and Beacon Tarn.

A grassy path climbs through bracken and passes to the right side of a stand of conifers before levelling out among bracken-clad rocky knolls. Soon **Beacon Tarn** comes into view. It's a fine sheet of water encircled by rocky knolls. The path descends slightly to its southern shores.

The official way continues along the western shoreline path, which,

although wetter underfoot, is easier. At the far end of the tarn a grass path climbs in a bracken-scattered hollow to arrive at a narrow col. The path now hugs the crag-fringed hillslopes on the right, descending to a marshy basin, where it levels off again. At the far end of the basin, at a spot marked by a cairn next to a wind-warped tree, the path angles right and eases down towards the marshy **Stable Harvey Moss**.

Among the wild, undulating terrain of the moss and the beiges, golds and reds of the moor grasses there's another blue tarn, known to some as Torver Tarn and to others as Throng Moss Reservoir (it's not named on current maps).

> The view is punctuated by rustic wooden electricity pylons, which somehow don't detract from its charm that much, and isolated thorn trees. But they're all bit part players on a stage dominated by the **Coniston Fells** beyond. To the left Dow Crag displays its cliffs and gullies; Coniston Old Man shows less crag but has a fine conical shape and Wetherlam's long lumpy ridge completes the scene.

Take a note here of the farmhouse (or the trees enshrouding it, in summer!) on the nearby pastured hillside (**Stable Harvey**) – that's where we're heading. Stay with the prominent narrow path, which veers left towards a large crag, beneath which it curves right to trace the foot of a low rock and grass ridge. The path fords Black Beck. Beyond this it climbs one of those knolls on the low ridge before joining a tarmac road climbing towards Stable Harvey farm.

Just before reaching its entrance gate turn left following a signed bridleway track. At the next junction of tracks take the higher right fork. Although both will do – they rejoin later – the right fork is usually drier underfoot.

The track veers left at a waymarker post and soon divides again. ◀ Take the right fork, which fords Mere Beck. The beck cuts a pleasant valley that will lead the route down to the Coniston road.

The path going straight ahead is the Torver link (see below).

A grass path descends the valley, which is now greener and with more trees and juniper bushes. It crosses Torver Beck before climbing to a roadside gate. Across the busy **A5084** (take care) a good track arcs gradually left and comes down to the shores of **Coniston Water** by the short jetty at **Sunny Bank**. A delightful and easy path takes the route along this tree-lined shoreline, past the launch landing station at Hoathwaite.

Coniston Water and the Sunny Bank Jetty

> Across the waters lies the grand mansion of **Brantwood**, once owned by John Ruskin, a renowned artist, poet, political thinker and art critic from the Victorian era. It is now owned by the National Trust and run as a museum dedicated to him.

The path veers left inland a little and passes through the Coniston Hall campsite using its access track.

> **Coniston Hall** is an impressive stone and slate building with four enormous chimneys and fine mullioned windows. It dates back to the 16th century and is owned by the National Trust.

Follow the lane from Coniston Hall but, just beyond the sailing club and farm outbuildings, leave it for a gravelly track on the right. This takes the route across fields to Lake Road, where you turn left into **Coniston** village.

Torver link

Just beyond the path's left turn towards Mere Beck (SD 280 922) the Torver link diverts from the official Coniston route. Instead of following the Cumbria Way down the valley of Mill Beck go straight on to cross the beck higher up. The path comes to and follows the shores of Torver Tarn/Throng Moss Reservoir (not named on current maps).

The path you need soon climbs above the shores but make sure you don't follow subsidiary paths to the hilltops – that hard-won ascent would have to be lost. Follow the path north over wild moorland before descending to a gate on the edge of access land. Beyond this an enclosed path leads down to the cottages by Mill Bridge (not named on OS Landranger maps – SD 285 932). Don't cross Torver Beck here but go through a gate to the left of the large former mill.

Through this an enclosed path takes you parallel to the beck at first before veering away left to a tarred farm lane near **Moor Farm**. Turn right along this and follow the lane out to a T-junction, where you turn right, passing Shepherd House caravan site before coming to the main road. Turn left into **Torver**.

The old mill from Mill Bridge

CONISTON

The Coniston Gondola

When they built Coniston village, they built it beneath a grand mountain that would share its name, and built it out of the rock hewn from that mountain. It's not chocolate-box pretty like Wordsworth's Grasmere but you can see why poet and philosopher John Ruskin settled here in 1871. The view across Coniston Water from his house at Brantwood (open Mar–Nov 10.30am–5pm; Nov–Mar 10.30am–4pm; www.brantwood.org.uk) shows the little village with its slate church, shops and cottages sheltering in lakeside pastures, with Coniston Old Man rearing up from the backyards in true alpine fashion: village and mountain are inseparable. Before his death, Ruskin declined to be buried in style at Westminster Abbey instead opting to be laid to rest in Coniston's St Andrew's churchyard. His grave is embellished with a fine cross made from Tilberthwaite green slate.

Coniston was powered by hydroelectricity from Church Beck during the 1930s but subsequent heavy taxation of the 1950s forced its inhabitants to return to the National Grid. However in 2007 another hydroelectric scheme adapted from the same site was commissioned and today supplies 300kw of power.

Donald Campbell brought fame to the lake, setting four of his seven world speed records here in the 1950s. Having set a seventh record (290mph) in Western Australia in 1964, he returned to Coniston Water three years later for further attempt. His boat, Bluebird K7, was seconds away from another record when its nose lifted and catapulted into the air at over 300mph, killing Campbell instantly. Donald Campbell is still the only person to hold both land and water speed records at the same time. Divers recovered his remains and the wreck of Bluebird in 2001. The boat has since been fully restored and is on display at the village's Ruskin Museum (open early Mar–early Nov, every day, 10.00am–5.30pm; early Nov–early Mar, Wed–Sun, 10.30am–3.30pm; www.ruskinmuseum.com).

If you have time, take a steam-powered gondola or a standard boat trip on Coniston Water (Coniston Pier, Lake Road, Tel: 015394 32733, www.nationaltrust.org.uk/gondola or Coniston Launch, Tel: 017687 75753; www.conistonlaunch.co.uk).

www.conistontic.org

STAGE 2
Coniston (or Torver) to Great Langdale

Start	bridge over Church Beck, Coniston (or Torver village)
Distance	11¾ miles (19km); 15¼ miles (24.5km) from Torver
Ascent	550m
Approx time	5–6 hours; 6–7 from Torver
Terrain	low wooded hills, country lane, low fell and river/lakeside path
Maps	OS Explorer OL6 & 7 South Western and South Eastern areas
Supplies	Torver: one shop with general supplies; Coniston: plenty of shops; Chapel Stile: one shop with general supplies
Variant	Bridleway shortcut near Colwith Force

The climb out of Coniston is a gentle one, over pastured hillsides, flecked with colourful gorse bushes and then by a playful beck. Throughout the early part of the day there are subtly changing views across the verdant fields and woods to the crags of the Yewdale Fells, a view enhanced in spring and autumn when the bracken appears as a fiery red blanket. Although the lake of Tarn Hows is artificial it's beautiful all the same, with wide views across its waters to the Langdale Pikes and Helvellyn.

Two waterfalls, Colwith Force and Skelwith Force, can be visited on the next section and both are torrential after periods of rain, but the best views of the day come beyond Skelwith when the route enters the great glacial valley of Great Langdale. Here the angular near-vertical crags of the Pikes tower above the gentle river and lake scenery.

Starting from Torver
The old Torver–Coniston railway track has been made into a trail and can be accessed 50m up the **A5084** or from the back of the Church Inn car park.

Starting from Coniston
Turn left along the old trackbed and follow it over the bridge spanning Torver Beck and through a cutting. Beyond a bridge bear left on a path to a minor road. Turn left along

STAGE 2 – CONISTON (OR TORVER) TO GREAT LANGDALE

this then left again on an access track passing to the left of **Hoathwaite Farm** and past the caravans to reach the lakeshore north of Hoathwaite Landing (SD 302 952). Turn left along the official Cumbria Way route past Coniston Hall and along the Lake Road.

From the bridge over Church Beck in the centre of the village go down Tilberthwaite Avenue, which passes to the left of St Andrew's church and to the right of the Crown Inn. Turn left at the junction signed Skelwith and Ambleside (Shepherd's Bridge Lane). Opposite to the school turn right over Shepherd's Bridge then turn immediately left through a gate by the cottage on the other side. The path follows **Yewdale Beck** for a

map continues on page 48

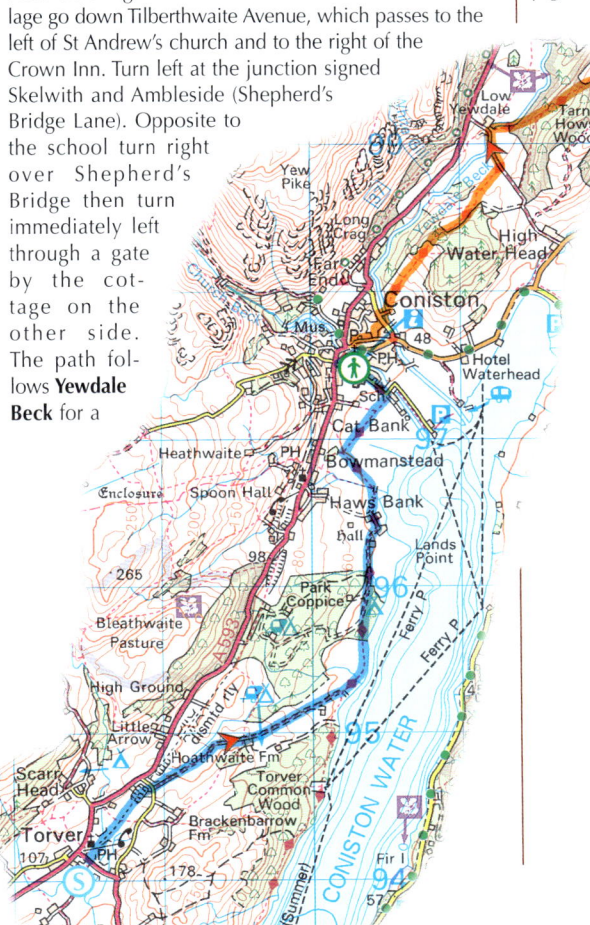

The old folly north of Coniston

short way before veering away slightly right and climbing sloping green pastures by a line of trees to reach an elaborate stone-built folly with castellated towers.

The **folly** was once used as a home for hunting hounds and has been restored by the National Trust. There are seats inside if the weather isn't so good and you need early refreshment.

When in bloom the gorse offers a fine foreground for the view back towards the village and lake.

Go through a gate to the left of the folly and follow the path climbing through trees with a fence to the right. Beyond another gate the path climbs gorse-scattered high pastures. ◀

Ignore the right fork path but carry on in the same direction to enter woodland through another gate. Beyond the woods the path enters more gorse scattered pasture, with woods and a dry-stone wall to the right.

Hereabouts you'll be enjoying the view to the left, which includes the magnificent **Yewdale Crags** with a narrow but impressive white-water cascade tumbling down the rocks to the oakwoods below.

The woodland perimeter wall, which runs parallel to the continuing path, angles right, uphill and ceases to

STAGE 2 – CONISTON (OR TORVER) TO GREAT LANGDALE

be of any guidance and at this point a faint track bisects the way. The path on the ground is very faint here but veer left a little bit (due north) – you should notice a gate beyond a couple of fine oak trees – that's where the path goes. A couple of waymarks offer reassurance. Beyond the gate the faint path goes along the middle of the next field to reach a trackside gate. Turn left beyond this, descending an enclosed stony track, which soon meets and runs alongside Yewdale Beck.

Just before the stone bridge taking the track across the beck go through a kissing gate on the right and follow a beckside path signed 'Tarn Hows'. Beyond another gate the path begins a climb through **Tarn Hows Wood**. It crosses a footbridge over a streamlet and continues the climb to the grounds of Tarn Hows Cottage.

A gravel path bypasses the pretty whitewashed cottage on the right and climbs to an access road above it. Climb out to a tarred lane. Turn left along the lane, which zigzags up the hillside to the nearest of the Tarn Hows National Trust **car parks**.

> Following the enclosure act of 1862 James Garth Marshall gained control of the what is now known as **Tarn Hows** and planted the area around the tarns with larch, pines and spruce. He then constructed a dam at Low Tarn to make the lake you see today. The area became part of the Monk Coniston estate, which stretched from Coniston to Skelwith Bridge. In 1929 Beatrix Potter bought the estate for £15,000 and sold the Tarn Hows area to the National Trust. She bequeathed the remaining part of the estate in her will.

Just past the car park take the track on the left and follow it round the north side of the tree-enshrouded tarn. At a three-way intersection of tracks turn left to follow the one signed 'Arnside and the Langdales'.

As you go through a wide gate, ignore the track climbing the hillside to the right but stay with the track going straight ahead, descending to meet a tarred lane from High

WALKING THE CUMBRIA WAY

map continues on page 53

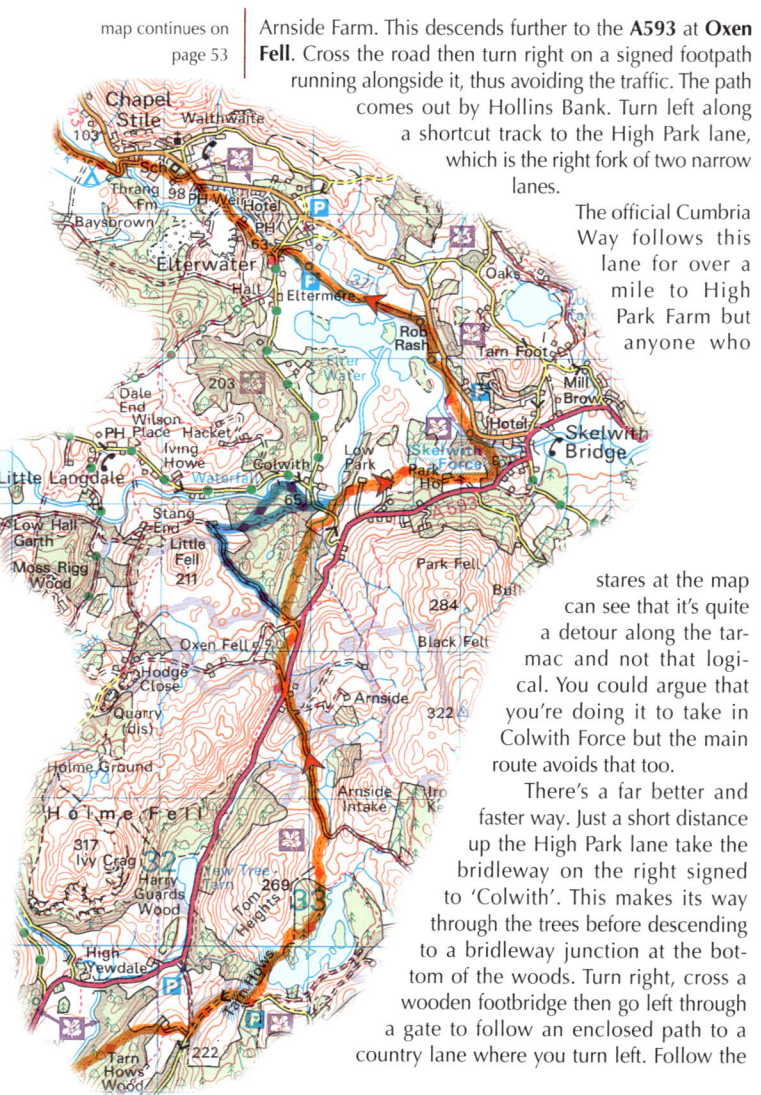

Arnside Farm. This descends further to the **A593** at **Oxen Fell**. Cross the road then turn right on a signed footpath running alongside it, thus avoiding the traffic. The path comes out by Hollins Bank. Turn left along a shortcut track to the High Park lane, which is the right fork of two narrow lanes.

The official Cumbria Way follows this lane for over a mile to High Park Farm but anyone who stares at the map can see that it's quite a detour along the tarmac and not that logical. You could argue that you're doing it to take in Colwith Force but the main route avoids that too.

There's a far better and faster way. Just a short distance up the High Park lane take the bridleway on the right signed to 'Colwith'. This makes its way through the trees before descending to a bridleway junction at the bottom of the woods. Turn right, cross a wooden footbridge then go left through a gate to follow an enclosed path to a country lane where you turn left. Follow the lane around a left hand bend to meet the official way again at a stile on the right (NY 331 030).

Official route
Follow the High Park lane to the nearside of High Park Farm, which does B&B. If you're hungry the farm also serves excellent scones, tea and bacon butties, in a tea garden if it's fine: if you're not, turn right along a gravel path across the fields and go through a gate into the woods. The right fork main path continues high up in the woods. Take the left fork on meeting a bridleway. This descends to a roadside stile by the Little Langdale lane at NY 330 030.

Turn right along the lane. After 90m go over a stile on the left hand side on the path signed 'to Skelwith Bridge' (NY 331 030).

Official variant taking in Colwith Force
The superior left fork path at the woodland edge east of High Park visits Colwith Force and descends, some places in slabbed steps, to the top of the falls. It then descends further past the base of the falls before continuing close to the river to meet the official route by the roadside stile.

Turn right along the lane. After 90m go over a stile on the left hand side on the path signed 'to Skelwith Bridge' (NY 331 030). This is where all the routes converge.

The clear path traverses a meadow before entering woodland where it climbs steep banks on steps to reach high pastures. A good winding path continues towards the houses at **Low Park**. After going through a gate to the right of the houses and crossing the access lane the route continues through a small gate and along a narrow enclosed ginnel. At the end of this a gravel path continues across high fields to a stile in a cross-wall. Beyond this the route comes to the courtyard of the Elterwater Park complex, where there's a B&B. On the other side a gravel path continues to the **Park House** cottages, which are passed on the right. Follow the access lane beyond but leave it where the lane veers right towards the road.

Colwith Force

STAGE 2 – CONISTON (OR TORVER) TO GREAT LANGDALE

River Brathay, Great Langdale and Wetherlam

A gravel left fork path continues and soon enters woodland and veers left. Take the next left fork signed 'Elterwater and Coniston' (the right fork goes to the road at Skelwith Bridge) and follow it down to cross a steel footbridge over the **River Brathay**.

Turn right for a there-and-back detour to see the **Skelwith Force** waterfall. Be careful on the rocks by the falls they can be slippery with the spray.

Turn left after the bridge on a wide, well-used path that follows the riverbank to the southern tip of **Elter Water**.

This beauty spot has a view across reed beds towards the **Langdale Pikes**, whose stature will grow with each step along the valley. From here their spectacular crags are tempered, not only by the lapping waters of the lakes but by woodland fringes and the low crusty-cragged ridges of Lingmoor Fell and Dow Bank.

The path enters more woodland before following the banks of **Great Langdale Beck** and passes Elterwater village's car park before coming to the road.

Elterwater comes from the Norse *elptarvatn* meaning 'swan lake' and you might well have seen migrating whooper swans on the lake earlier. It's a grand little place and the Britannia Inn, which has a pleasant outdoor seating area overlooking the village green, makes a good place for a refreshment stop.

Stage 2A joins the route here.

◀ Turn left across the road bridge here, then immediately right on a cul-de-sac. When the lane comes to a large sealed mine entrance leave it for a path on the right, which descends to the riverside overlooking the back of the Langdale Hotel and Spa.

The **Langdale Hotel and Spa** has been built on the site of the old gunpowder works, which thrived from 1824 until 1929. Six active water wheels powered the mills where the powder was ground and at its peak 80 men were employed here. After its closure in 1929 most of the buildings were burned to the ground, removing the possibility of any remaining gunpowder causing accidents.

Beyond the large complex go across the footbridge spanning Great Langdale Beck and turn right to emerge on the road by the Wainwright Inn at **Chapel Stile**. Follow the road left in front of the inn then fork left on a signed track, which joins a narrow lane behind the village school. Turn left along the lane to pass in front of the cottages of Thrang Garth.

Turn left as the track approaches the Great Langdale road to pass behind more houses, then turn sharp left to cross a stone bridge over Great Langdale Beck. Turn right between the southern bank and the flat fields of the **Baysbrown** farm campsite. Unless you intend to camp ignore a concrete road on the left heading towards the farm but instead continue with the beckside track.

On the approach to a footbridge the track veers left to pass **Oak Howe**. Turn right above the barn to follow a right fork path signed 'New Dungeon Ghyll', passing beneath the slopes of **Lingmoor Fell**. The majestic ramparts of the Langdale Pikes look ever more impressive.

For the most part the rugged undulating path runs alongside a stone wall to the right, but at an old sheepfold it goes through a gate in the wall and the engineered path that follows descends to **Side House**. Turn right on the farm's access track to re-cross the beck and reach the road opposite to the Stickle Barn car park just left of the **New Dungeon Ghyll Hotel**.

The official route goes through the car park, staggered to the left across the road and turns left

The Langdale Pikes from the path near Oak Howe

New Dungeon Ghyll beneath the Langdale Pikes

immediately before the toilet block. It climbs to join a path from the right and, through a gate, comes to a junction of paths beneath Stickle Ghyll. Take the rough bouldery path on the left. This follows a wall on the left then take the lower left fork at the next junction – the upper right fork is the path up to Loft Crag and Pike o' Stickle. The path comes to a junction above the **Old Dungeon Ghyll Hotel**. Descend left to go there or to the campsite beyond.

Quick route between the hotels

There's a much easier and quicker route to the Old Dungeon Ghyll Hotel. Take the first signed footpath on the left from the Stickle Barn car park and follow it across a field and by a secluded whitewashed cottage. Beyond the cottage the path crosses a footbridge over a stream on the right and continues west across fields to draw alongside the north bank of Great Langdale Beck. It then roughly follows the beck to come out at a gate behind the car park by the Old Dungeon Ghyll Hotel.

STAGE 2A
Torver to Great Langdale – mountain route

Start	Torver
Distance	15½ miles (25km)
Ascent	1130m
Approx time	8–9 hours
Maps	OS Explorer OL6 & 7 South Western and South Eastern areas
Supplies	Torver: one shop with general supplies; Chapel Stile: one shop with general supplies

This stage starts easily, passing campsites, cottages and quarry pits before coming upon Goat's Water, whose dark waters are dwarfed by the shadowy climbers' cliffs, buttresses and gullies of Dow Crag. A steady climb takes the route to Goat's Hawse, where you look across to new mountainscapes encompassing Seathwaite Tarn, Harter Fell and Grey Friar.

The hard work is done and a splendid promenade of a path rakes across the high eastern slopes of Brim Fell to reach the ridge at Levers Hawse before climbing to the high point of the day on Swirl How's summit.

What follows is an equally delightful descent into Little Langdale by way of Great Carrs and Wet Side Edge. Easy end-of-the-day paths continue for a couple of miles to join the official route at Elterwater.

A fingerpost signed to Torver High Common shows the start of the path by the north side of the Wilsons Arms. A gate at the back of the car park leads to an enclosed footpath. At a four-way path junction beneath a whitewashed farmhouse turn right on an enclosed track, then take the left fork track, which soon joins a narrow tarred lane passing the farm and campsite of Scarr Head. The lane becomes a track and climbs past the **Tranearth** climbing hut before coming to the disused Banishead Quarry, where the track comes through a gate to a walled enclosure. Now go through the gate on the far right of the enclosure and through another gate on the right cross the bridge over Torver Beck. A track now continues parallel

The actual Goat's Water path junction is about 50m west of the path junction marked on the OS Explorer map.

to the beck before rounding a large quarry pit with a waterfall plunging into the lake that has formed at the base of the pit.

There are a couple of tracks that begin at a stream crossing (SD 276 963). The left fork meets the **Walna Scar Road** (track) at the intersection point for the path for Goat's Water (SD 274 965). ◄ The slightly quicker route veers right for a few paces across wet ground then climbs grassy hillside to meet the Walna Scar Road at SD 275 965 – this keeps all stream hollows to the left.

The continuing path climbs beneath the slopes of Coniston Old Man and the terrain becomes more bouldery. The buttresses and gullies of **Dow Crag**, usually sullen and sunless, form a moody, impressive backdrop. The path draws up to and runs alongside the shores of **Goat's Water** before climbing to the large cairn on Goat's Hawse.

map continues on page 58

New mountainscapes come into view. **Seathwaite Tarn** peeps out from behind Dow Crag's declining grass slopes, with the pyramidal **Harter Fell** and the dome-like **Grey Friar** dominating beyond the shoreline.

Turn right and climb onto the slopes of Brim Fell but leave this path for a faint (at first) left fork path, which rakes NNE across the mountain slopes to meet the ridge path at **Levers Hawse**. Although it omits Coniston Old Man and Brim Fell this path is superior in every way.

Coniston Old Man is the most popular of this compact group of fells lying on the southern edge of Lakeland. Rising to

Goat's Water from Goat's Hawse

803m it lies on the end of a ridge thrown out by Swirl How. Most guidebooks will tell you that the Old Man is the highest peak but Harvey Maps have thrown this into confusion with their measurement of Swirl How at 804m.

Should you want to visit the Old Man don't take the left fork above Goat's Hawse but instead keep right along a good path all the way to the ridge just short of the Coniston Old Man's summit. To rejoin the main mountain route retrace your steps but this time stay on the ridge path over Brim Fell before descending to Levers Hawse.

At Levers Hawse a good stony path climbs first to **Great How Crags** then to **Swirl How**, which has a large beehive cairn on its summit.

From Swirl How head west following the path that rounds the top of Broad Slack, with fine cliffs to the right. The path soon comes to the summit of **Great Carrs**, where you can look back to Swirl How and all the walkers on the **Prison Band**. The path descends to **Little Carrs**, then

WALKING THE CUMBRIA WAY

Swirl How's summit cairn

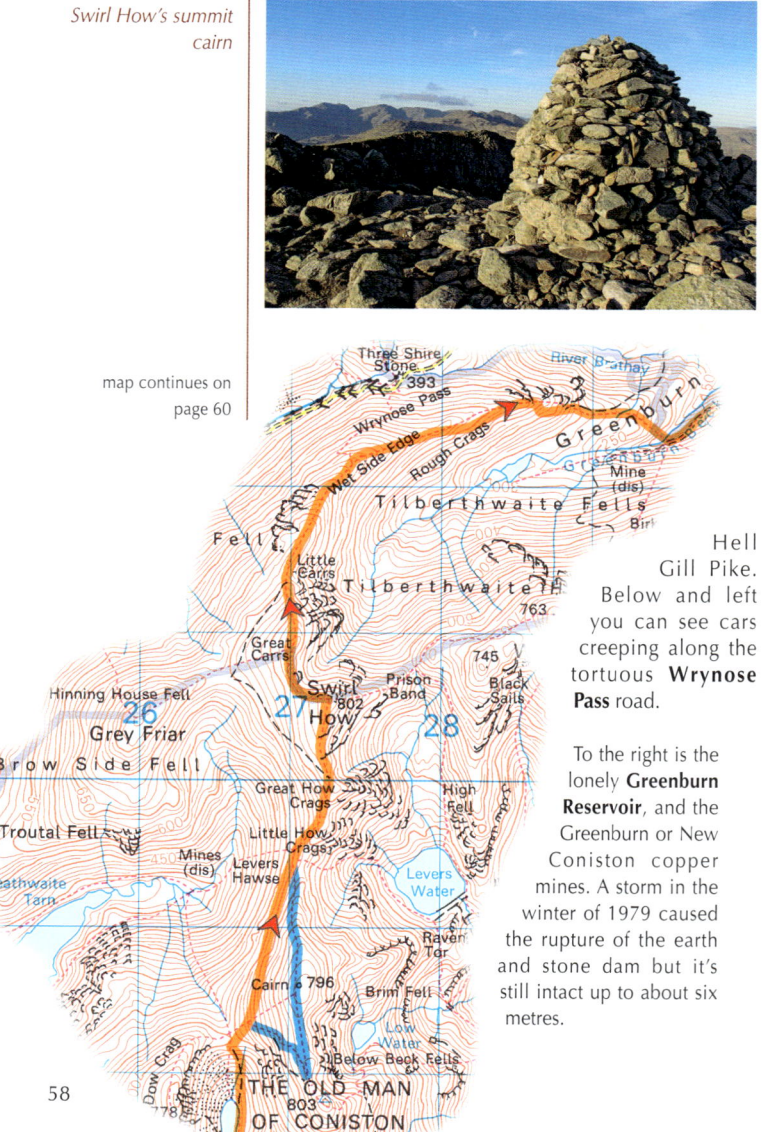

map continues on page 60

Hell Gill Pike. Below and left you can see cars creeping along the tortuous **Wrynose Pass** road.

To the right is the lonely **Greenburn Reservoir**, and the Greenburn or New Coniston copper mines. A storm in the winter of 1979 caused the rupture of the earth and stone dam but it's still intact up to about six metres.

Stage 2A – Torver to Great Langdale – mountain route

MINING ON THE CONISTON FELLS

The Banishead Quarry Pit beneath Coniston Old Man

The Coniston Fells have a great presence. The ice ages chiselled masterpieces in their crag faces and corries, but since Roman times these mountains have become rural factories – even the main valley leading into them is known as Coppermines Valley.

The Coniston slate mines have been worked intensively since the 13th century. The main locations are in the Coppermines area, Tilberthwaite and the Brossen/Bursting Stone area, south east of the Old Man. They were underground workings, with the exception of Low Brandy Crag, which was excavated into an opencast quarry in the 1980s by Burlington Stone. Today just two remain operational: Low Brandy Crag, which supplies blue slate and Brossen Stone, which supplies pale green slate.

Large-scale mining for copper began some 400 years ago, when Queen Elizabeth I sent in a team of German miners to work with hand tools on the veins that surfaced on rock outcrops. The hard rhyolite rock of the Borrowdale Volcanic group made the drilling difficult and slow. In the 1640s activity declined, partly due to the destruction of the Keswick smelting works during the Civil War. It increased for a short period in the middle of the 18th century, when the Macclesfield Mining Company took over. They built a water wheel for pumping and used gunpowder to ease further excavation to levels over 100m.

The industry reached its peak by the mid-19th century after mining engineer John Taylor and his mine manager John Barrett took control and ordered the drilling of deeper shafts, the construction of access and drainage levels and a system of leats that transported water to where it was needed. A railway between Furness and Coniston made distribution of the ore for smelting easier. By then the shafts had reached over 500m beneath the surface. Gradually the industry declined, with the maintenance costs increasing to unsustainable proportions. By the 1940s all activity had ceased. Today, most of the deep shafts of the copper mines are abandoned, flooded and dangerous – it would be difficult to tell whether you were standing on the floor of the pit or trusting your fate to a rotting debris-covered timber platform.

The descent from Little Carrs is a gradual one along **Wet Side Edge** (which is not particularly wet). The path you want starts to veer to the right-hand side of the ridge as the route approaches the great crags overlooking Wrynose Bottom. Faint at first in the upper reaches, it descends as a grassy passage between the rocks, then turns left as a clear path through bracken. It then flattens out in a boggy area but you'll be able to pick out the slightly darker swath that is the path. This passes a couple of low crags before descending steeply as a grass path through bracken.

Keep right of a wall corner to descend to a footbridge over **Greenburn Beck**. Climb the far banks and turn left along a stony mine track. This descends past the cottages of High and Low Hall Garth. Turn left through a kissing gate beyond the second cottage, used by the Yorkshire Ramblers as a base, and descend to cross Slater's Bridge.

Climb on a narrow path up hill pastures. Beyond the first gate the path becomes a stony track, and beyond the second by High Birk How Farm, turn left along another stony track, which comes out onto the Wrynose Pass road. Turn left for a few paces then right along a lane signed 'Ambleside – Challenging Route'. The lane becomes a stony track beyond **Dale End** farm. Beyond a gate it enters and descends through Sawrey Wood. Take the right fork at the next junction. This continues the descent to the Elterwater road by the **Eltermere** Hotel. Turn left along the road, passing the youth hostel before meeting the official way at the bridge over **Great Langdale Beck**.

Now follow Stage 2 to the Old Dungeon Ghyll Hotel.

STAGE 3
Great Langdale to Keswick

Start	Old Dungeon Ghyll Hotel
Distance	16 miles (25.5km)
Ascent	645m
Approx time	8–9 hours
Terrain	stiff climb to Stake Pass, rough in places in Langstrath, woodland and lakeside paths in Borrowdale
Maps	OS Explorer OL4 & 6 North Western and South Western areas
Supplies	Portinscale has a shop/post office; Keswick has a wide range of shops, including a large Booths supermarket

Today is a watershed day. So far the Cumbria Way has chosen pretty routes through valleys by lakes and tarns and across low wooded hillsides. Today it tackles the high mountain pass barring the way out of Great Langdale into Borrowdale. It's wild country and Langstrath, the valley that leads you into Borrowdale, is uninhabited and just as wild. But the scenery is magnificent from the start, when you walk above the ancient fields of Mickleden towards the head of the valley where the crags of Bowfell and Rossett Pike rear up from the bouldery riverside.

The winding path to Stake Pass is steep but short and soon you're walking through the undulating moraines and contemplating the equally steep winding path down into Langstrath. The greenery returns as you turn the corner towards Stonethwaite and you enter the lush rain-enhanced landscapes of Borrowdale. The paths around Derwent Water are a delight and the pastel-coloured smooth slopes of Skiddaw beckon you on towards Keswick and the prospect of a bar meal and a comfortable bed for the night.

Return to the path behind the **Old Dungeon Ghyll Hotel** and this time beyond the first gate turn left on a wide path, with a drystone wall on the left and the steep rugged slopes of Raven Crag on the right.

After about 800m the spur known as **the Band** divides Great Langdale with the combe of **Oxendale** on the left and that of **Mickleden** ahead. The path gently

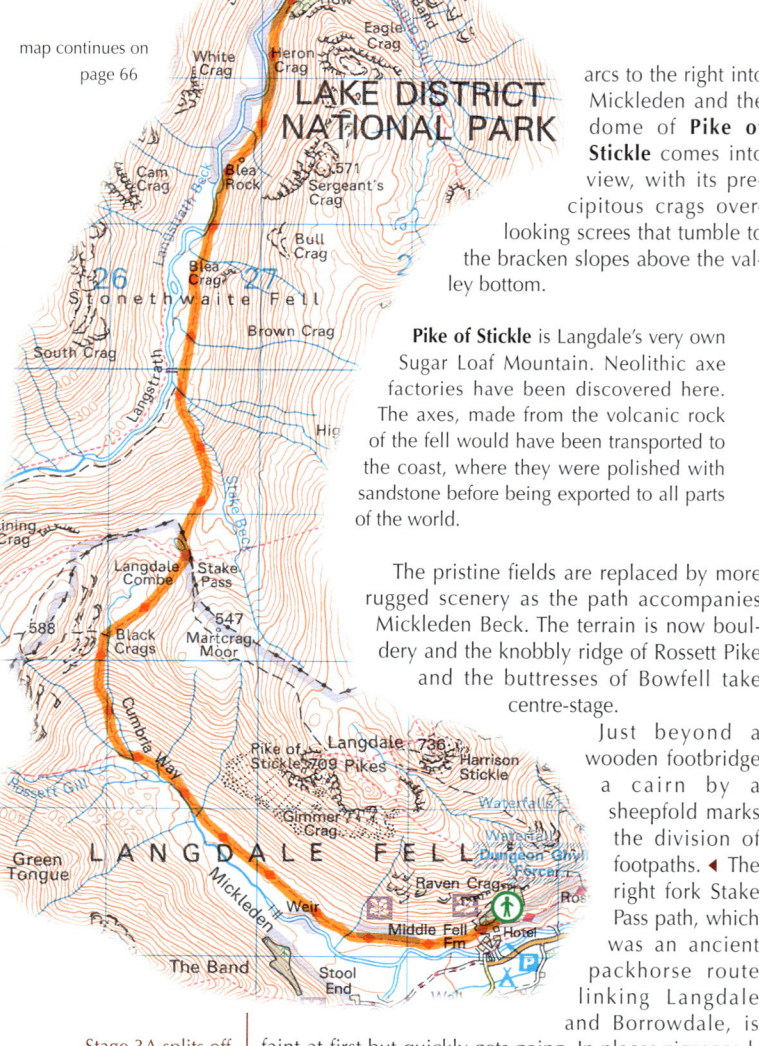

arcs to the right into Mickleden and the dome of **Pike of Stickle** comes into view, with its precipitous crags overlooking screes that tumble to the bracken slopes above the valley bottom.

Pike of Stickle is Langdale's very own Sugar Loaf Mountain. Neolithic axe factories have been discovered here. The axes, made from the volcanic rock of the fell would have been transported to the coast, where they were polished with sandstone before being exported to all parts of the world.

The pristine fields are replaced by more rugged scenery as the path accompanies Mickleden Beck. The terrain is now bouldery and the knobbly ridge of Rossett Pike and the buttresses of Bowfell take centre-stage.

Just beyond a wooden footbridge a cairn by a sheepfold marks the division of footpaths. ◄ The right fork Stake Pass path, which was an ancient packhorse route linking Langdale and Borrowdale, is faint at first but quickly gets going. In places zigzagged, the path has been sympathetically inlaid with stone and meanders, hardly visible from below, among more

Stage 3A splits off here.

Looking up the Stake Pass from junction of low and high routes in Mickleden

boulders and bracken. Up ahead you'll see the cascades of Stake Gill. After passing the upper cascades of the beck the path levels off to reach **Langdale Combe**.

The hummocks of **Langdale Combe** are moraines from the last ice age. To the right the sulking grass slopes of **Martcrag Moor** show that the Langdales have a side very different from those boastful Great Langdale buttresses.

A narrow but clear path weaves between the moraines, generally NE towards the top of **Stake Pass**. On the approach to the cairn on the col ignore the path doubling back right (it climbs to Pike of Stickle) and the one to the left (going to Esk Hause).

The cairn marks the **watershed** and the top of Stake Pass. Rivers and streams in front of you flow northwards, eventually into the Solway Firth, while behind you they flow into Morecambe Bay.

The continuing path heads NNE from the cairn and passes beneath a shallow windswept tarn, which you won't see unless you climb a few feet up the grassy banks to your left. It then arcs slightly right (NNW) and descends gently at first. But then Langstrath opens up and you're looking down on this wild cavernous hollow, the longest uninhabited valley in the Lake District.

The path descends in engineered zigzags down steep slopes. **Stake Beck** (not to be confused with Stake Gill on the Langdale side) appears from the right. The cascading white waters have gouged a fine little rocky gorge dotted with trees.

At the bottom of the slope the path crosses a footbridge over Stake Beck before continuing down the valley with **Langstrath Beck** on the left. You'll see another footbridge over Langstrath Beck and the path on the other side is usable as far as Stonethwaite. The official Cumbria Way, however, stays this side, picking its way over boulder-strewn ground. Ahead the fine buttresses of **Cam Crag** dominate the scenery.

Falls on Langstrath Beck

As you pass beneath the crag and through a gate in a stone wall onto some marshy ground watch out for some rocky outcrops by the river, for hereabouts the beck passes through an attractive but small rocky gorge known as **Blackmoss Pot** – it's only a short detour.

The path continues past **Sergeant's Crag**, beneath which it goes over a ladder stile and continues with a wire fence on the left. The going is a little intricate across bouldery ground.

If you're stopping at Stonethwaite you could cross the beck using the footbridge at NY 272 126, otherwise it's best to stay on this side of the valley. Many trees now line the river and ahead you can see the convergence of Langstrath and Greenup Gill.

This area is known as **Smithymire Island**, a place where the monks of Furness Abbey used to smelt iron ore, which was transported by packhorse down Langstrath from Ore Gap.

The path crosses **Greenup Gill** on a wooden footbridge and climbs to a gate, beyond which you turn left. The Cumbria Way now shares its route with Wainwright's Coast to Coast Walk, albeit in opposite directions.

Looking back up Greenup Gill you cannot but be impressed by the powerful ramparts of **Eagle Crag**. To your left the river is now known as Stonethwaite Beck and flows in a series of fine cataracts and waterfalls.

Opposite the Stonethwaite **campsite** the path goes through a gate, where it joins a walled track dividing the river pastures and the tree-cloaked hillsides. You will be able to see the village of **Stonethwaite** on the far banks and Stonethwaite bridge offers a last chance to cross before Rosthwaite.

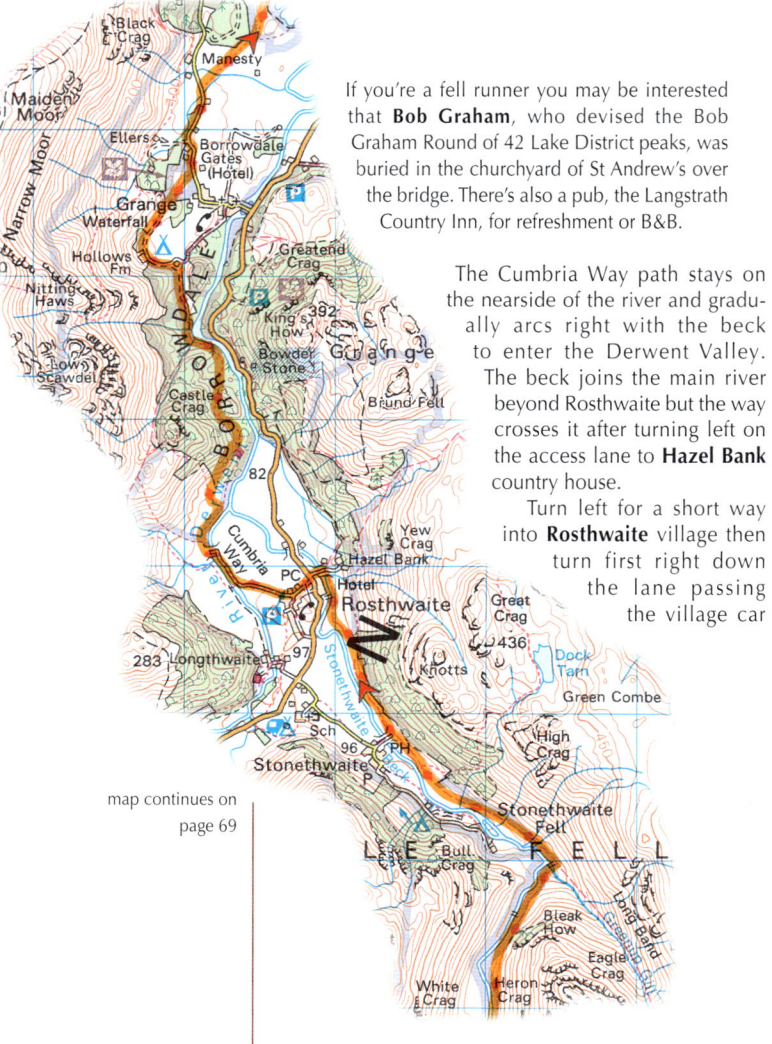

If you're a fell runner you may be interested that **Bob Graham**, who devised the Bob Graham Round of 42 Lake District peaks, was buried in the churchyard of St Andrew's over the bridge. There's also a pub, the Langstrath Country Inn, for refreshment or B&B.

The Cumbria Way path stays on the nearside of the river and gradually arcs right with the beck to enter the Derwent Valley. The beck joins the main river beyond Rosthwaite but the way crosses it after turning left on the access lane to **Hazel Bank** country house.

Turn left for a short way into **Rosthwaite** village then turn first right down the lane passing the village car

Stage 3A joins here.

park. ◀ Pass between the Flock-in Café and Yew Tree Farm (B&B) and continue on a walled track to the River Derwent. Ignore the stepping-stones here. The track

map continues on page 69

STAGE 3 – GREAT LANGDALE TO KESWICK

now follows the near bank then crosses on the New Bridge before turning right and following the far bank. Go through the right of two gates about 100m from the bridge and continue on a clear track.

Contrary to what is marked on the map, now take the clearer left fork track by a tree-enshrouded knoll. Unless

Castle Crag

River Derwent at Gowder Dub near Castle Crag

you want to climb **Castle Crag** ignore the upper path to the left near the crown of the bend but instead continue to the beautiful High Hows Wood. Here the path climbs to an area of cairns and quarry spoil heaps and goes through a gap in a cross wall. At GR NY 252161 there's a 3-way path intersection. Take the middle path, which slants up left, then double back right to a waymarking fingerpost. Follow the path signed to Grange. This heads north to another gap in a stone cross-wall, after which the path descends to the right before winding down to the river's edge at Gowder Dub. ◄

> This beauty spot is a great place for a picnic.

After being joined on the left by a bridleway from Seatoller the path veers away from the river. You'll often see campers in the woodland to your left, the outlying pitches of Hollows Farm. Next the way passes a narrow sliver of campsite pastureland behind a wall on the right and tucked beneath the wooded knoll of Homecrag Wood. An access track joins in from the pastures. Through a gateway take the left fork track, then join a lane to **Hollows Farm**.

Follow a track through the farmyard, and across low bracken-clad hillslopes, beneath woodland at first. ◄

> This section is particularly beautiful with the crags of Nitting Haws towering above the route to the left and the beautiful wooded crag-fringed valley of Troutdale to the right.

On reaching the perimeter wall of High Close Wood turn right and go through a gate. From here a good path winds down the hillside scattered with thorn trees and with the village of Grange below you. It descends to the road by the **Borrowdale Gates Hotel**.

Turn left along the road. Just beyond the crossing of Ellers Beck turn right through double gates and follow the path by the beck. The beck eventually meanders away right but the path maintains its north-east direction across rough pasture then by a forest plantation.

> Stage 3A splits off right here.

Just beyond a gate at the entrance to Derwent Water's flood plain (NY 254 186), bear left alongside the wall. ◄ Take the right fork path beyond some duckboarding to reach a popular engineered path from Lodore and turn left along it. ◄ Duckboards traverse the wettest areas as the path rounds **Great Bay** to enter the woodlands of Manesty Park.

> You'll be able to see this path clearly and there are several pathways to it.

STAGE 3 – GREAT LANGDALE TO KESWICK

Hugh Walpole, author of the *Herries Chronicle* series of books, which were set in the Lake District, lived nearby at Brackenburgh until his death in 1941. He is buried at St John's Church in Keswick.

After coming to the shoreline at **Abbot's Bay** the path turns inland and comes to a surfaced lane at a cottage. Turn right along it, passing the tip of Brandelhow Bay to reach the whitewashed house of the same name. Pass in front of the house and head for the gravel shores of Brandelhow Bay. Across the lake the mountains of Skiddaw and Blencathra captivate the scene.

Follow the path around the headland, past the High Brandelhow landing stage and beneath a beautiful woodland canopy of oak trees.

At Victoria Bay you'll come across a great wooden cupped hand. Known as **Entrust** and placed here in 2002, the sculpture commemorates the centenary

Entrust sculpture on the shores of Derwent Water

of the first purchase of land made by the National Trust, here in Brandelhow Woods. Princess Louise, daughter of Queen Victoria, opened the wood to the public.

Just beyond the Low Brandelhow landing stage go through a gate and take the inland left hand fork with a low grassy headland to your right. Through another gate the path joins a tarred access lane, which skirts the buildings of the **Hawes End** Outdoor Centre. After passing the entrance and car park to the centre ignore two right turns, but just beyond the second, a private drive, go right through a small gate onto a gravel path signed 'to Portinscale'. This continues through woodland at first, then crosses a field back into woodland. It eventually reaches **Lingholm**.

Lingholm is a fine mansion where Beatrix Potter spent many summer holidays. She whiled away the hours sketching in the gardens, also the woods you've just walked through and the red squirrels that still thrive here were the inspiration for her book *The Tale of Squirrel Nutkin*.

STAGE 3 – GREAT LANGDALE TO KESWICK

KESWICK

19th-century poet, art critic and political thinker John Ruskin, a frequent visitor to these parts, once said that Keswick was almost too beautiful to live in and that the view from Friar's Crag on Derwent Water was one of the three finest views in Europe.

This little market town is perfectly sited between the lakes of Derwent Water and Bassenthwaite, and sheltered beneath the serenely smooth and well-contoured slopes of Skiddaw. Its situation has inspired artists, writers, poets and philosophers to come here in numbers. Samuel Taylor Coleridge moved here with his family in 1800 in order to be near his great friend, William Wordsworth, and he was joined at Greta Hall three years later at by his brother-in-law, Robert Southey. Southey was Poet Laureate for 30 years until his death in 1843.

The town's origins were at Great Crosthwaite to the north-west of the current town centre, where St Kentigern founded his church in AD553. Canon Rawnsley, an influential figure and one of the pioneers of the National Trust movement, served as vicar here between 1883 and 1917.

Although the name Keswick means the place of cheese – cheese fairs were held here until the 1900s – early local industry was largely based on wool and leather. The town was granted a market charter in 1276. The 19th-century Moot Hall in the centre of the wide Main Street, where the markets are still held, has also been used as a prison and a town hall over the years. These days it houses the tourist information office.

The mining of graphite at Seathwaite in Borrowdale gave rise to Keswick's pencil-making industry – you can learn more about it at the town's pencil museum (Cumberland Pencil Museum, Southey Works, Keswick;

> open 9.30am–5pm; Tel: 017687 73626; www.pencilmuseum.co.uk). The Cockermouth, Keswick and Penrith Railway came to Keswick in 1865. It linked the main London and North Western Railway at Penrith to the coast of Cumbria via the Cockermouth and Workington Railway. Victorian tourists came from all over the country to see this land of lakes and poets. Sadly, the line closed in 1972 but you will get to see it on the Cumbria Way as you pass the old station on your way out of town.
>
> Other things to see: Keswick Museum Fitz Park (Station Road), open 10am–5pm, Tel: 017687 73263, www.keswickmuseum.org.uk; Theatre by the Lake (Lakeside), (great shows and a nice place to eat), Tel: 017687 74411, www.theatrebythelake.com; Derwentwater Launches (Lake Road), operating mid-Mar–end Nov, Tel: 017687 72263, www.keswick-launch.co.uk; Friar's Crag (great beauty spot as recommended by John Ruskin, NY 263 223 – a lovely evening stroll beyond the Keswick Launch landing stage).
>
> **www.keswick.org**

Turn left along Lingholm's access drive but where this turns left go straight on along a path signed to Keswick and Portinscale.

At the next junction both routes are usable, but the best one is the right fork track, which descends to the café and landing stage at **Nichol End**. ◄ The left fork route climbs through the woods of Fawe Park before descending to the Portinscale Road. Both routes meet at the point where the Nichol End access road meets the Portinscale Road.

Here you can get the biggest and best cherry scones you've ever tasted.

Take the access lane up left to reach a road leading north (right) into the village of **Portinscale**. Where the main road turns left go straight ahead to pass the large Derwentwater Hotel. Once across the bridge over the River Derwent turn right on a popular path across the fields to Keswick. The path converges with the banks of the River Greta, a tributary of the Derwent, as it emerges onto Main Street not far from the town centre.

Turn right along the street, over the bridge and keep going past the shops to reach the market square, where you'll come to this fine old Moot Hall, the official centre of the town.

Stage 3 – Great Langdale to Keswick

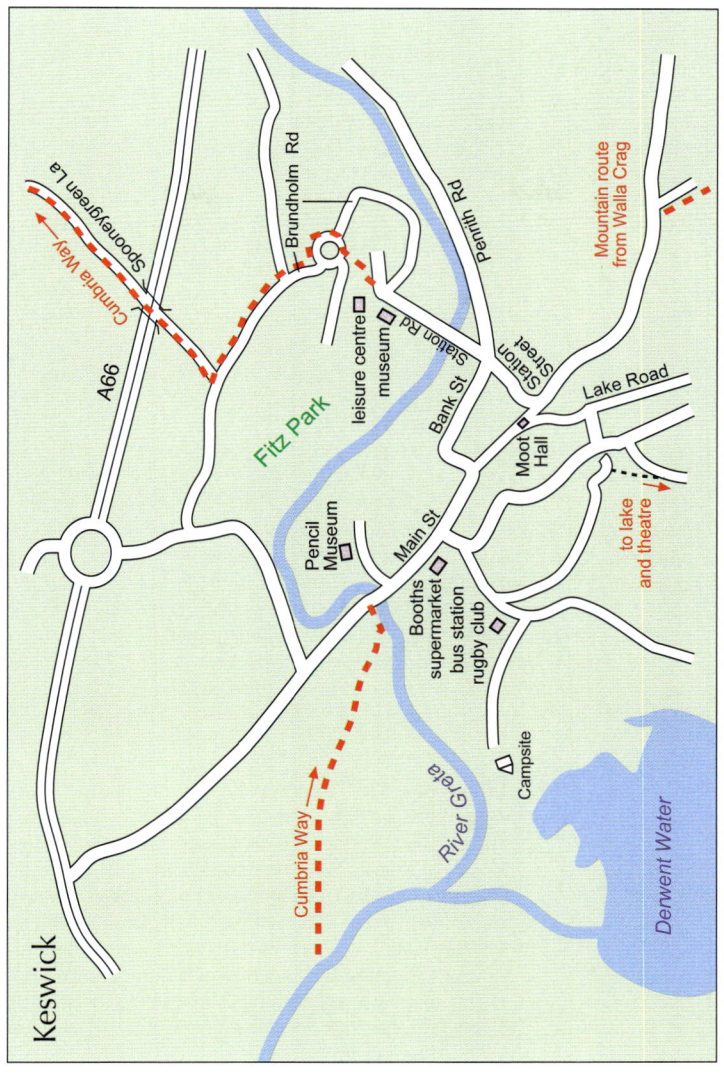

STAGE 3A
Great Langdale to Keswick – mountain route

Start	Old Dungeon Ghyll Hotel
Distance	17½ miles (28km); 18½ miles (29.5km) with Bowfell
Ascent	1430m; 1620m with Bowfell
Approx time	9–10 hours
Terrain	Steep climbs out of Mickleden, rough mountain paths on Glaramara, and final sting in the tail at Walla Crag (which can be avoided by diverting to official route at Rosthwaite)
Maps	OS Explorer OL4 & 6 North Western and South Western areas
Supplies	Keswick has a wide range of shops, including a large Booths supermarket

The mountain route takes you closer to the majestic crags of Bowfell as it climbs towards Esk Hawse. Allen Crags and Glaramara offer up a mountaintop challenge. The undulating paths couldn't be classified as promenades like those on the Coniston ridges but they do provide wonderful, ever-changing views of the surrounding mountains, and the way Borrowdale opens up on the descent from Thornythwaite Fell is a joy to behold. You could be forgiven for diverting to the official route round Derwent Water at the end of a long day but that would be missing the best view on the whole route – the one from Walla Crag. (Another solution would be to break your journey at Rosthwaite instead and tackle Walla Crag the next morning.)

Follow Stage 3 to the cairn at the bottom of the path leading up to **Stake Pass**. Here take the left fork with **Rossett Gill** on your left. The path climbs steadily across the low slopes of Rossett Pike then crosses the gill. The path, sometimes slabbed, begins a series of zigzags on craggy slopes then comes to a high pass, between **Bowfell** and **Rossett Pike**. From here it descends towards the outflow at the north-eastern corner of beautiful Angle Tarn, deeply set in a grassy bowl beneath the crags of **Hanging Knotts**. You can look down the outflow gill into the deep valley of **Langstrath**.

STAGE 3A – GREAT LANGDALE TO KESWICK – MOUNTAIN ROUTE

WHO'S FOR BOWFELL?

Bowfell is one of Lakeland's most majestic mountains, a powerful pyramid of rock, lording it over Great Langdale; and the Cumbria Way walker, who turns to the valley of Langstrath for the shelter of Borrowdale. And yet the Way gets so close it might just be worth including Bowfell in the itinerary. Okay, it does make the day a big one, but if any walker really wanted to bag this mighty fell they could shorten the day to finish at Seatoller or Rosthwaite. Including Bowfell in this stage adds 1 mile in distance and 190m in ascent.

Starting at the **Old Dungeon Ghyll Hotel** make your way back to the main road, turn right along it to the first bend, then take the access lane to **Stool End** farm. Beyond a gate at the far side of the farmyard follow a wall-side path forking left before climbing on a right fork path up the spur of the **Band**. The engineered path stays mainly to the south of the crest. On reaching a grassy plateau take the left fork, which soon climbs again up to a high pass at **Three Tarns**. The Scafells can be seen across the shallow pools and the head of Eskdale, while Bowfell's south face, the Bowfell Links, boasts a fierce crag face broken up by nine gullies.

The path from the pass climbs right then arcs left towards Bowfell's bouldery summit. Ignore a right fork path, which would take you to the Climbers' Traverse. On reaching the summit you may wish to explore the great crags and slabs of the eastern edge before continuing NNW on the main path, which descends among rocks to the west of the crest before veering left to **Ore Gap**.

From here the path climbs steadily to a second but only slightly less spectacular peak, **Esk Pike**. Descend from here to the pass of **Esk Hause**, where you'll come to a route intersection. Take the path doubling back right before curving left to descend to a cross-shaped shelter at the foot of **Allen Crags**. Here you join the main mountain route from Rossett Gill on the climb to Allen Crags.

After climbing further, descend to cross Allencrags Gill and climb again on a wide path which comes to the unnamed pass between the rocky **Esk Pike** (left) and Allen Crags (right) – **Esk Hause** lies above you to the left. You'll see a cross-shaped wall shelter ahead and a cairn just to the right of it. The cairn marks the start of the Allen Crags path wanted for this route.

WALKING THE CUMBRIA WAY

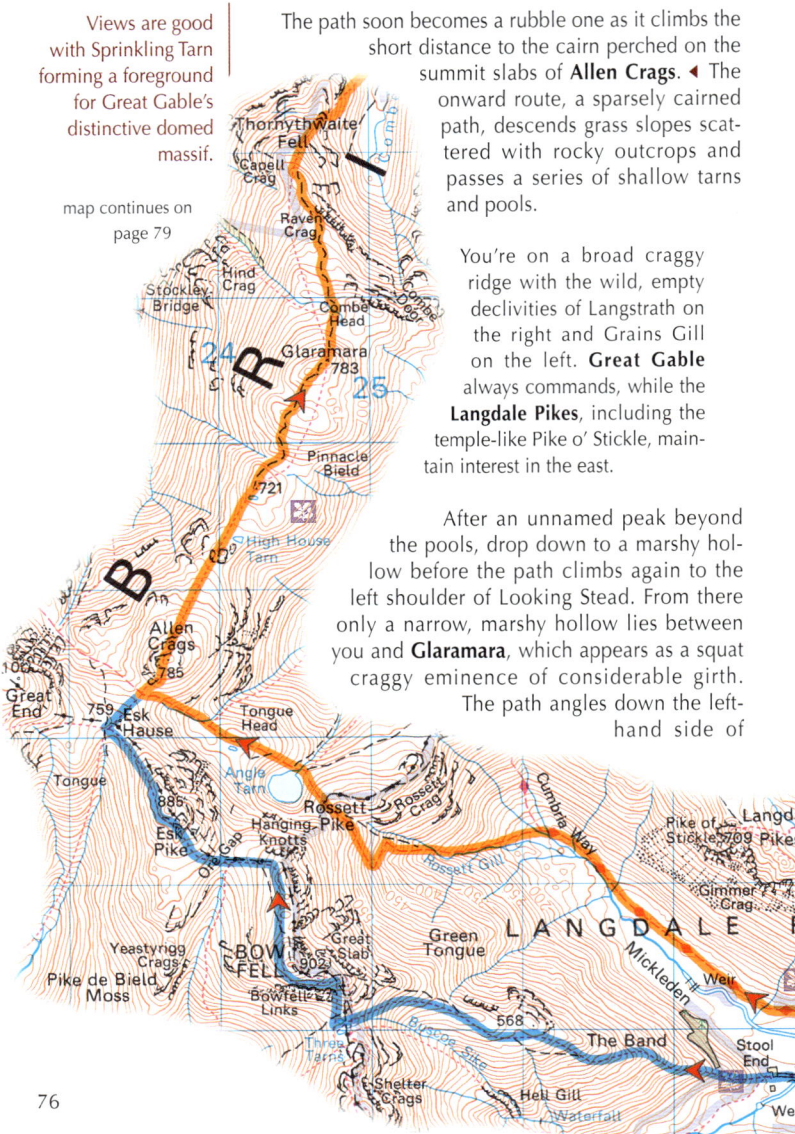

Views are good with Sprinkling Tarn forming a foreground for Great Gable's distinctive domed massif.

map continues on page 79

The path soon becomes a rubble one as it climbs the short distance to the cairn perched on the summit slabs of **Allen Crags**. ◄ The onward route, a sparsely cairned path, descends grass slopes scattered with rocky outcrops and passes a series of shallow tarns and pools.

You're on a broad craggy ridge with the wild, empty declivities of Langstrath on the right and Grains Gill on the left. **Great Gable** always commands, while the **Langdale Pikes**, including the temple-like Pike o' Stickle, maintain interest in the east.

After an unnamed peak beyond the pools, drop down to a marshy hollow before the path climbs again to the left shoulder of Looking Stead. From there only a narrow, marshy hollow lies between you and **Glaramara**, which appears as a squat craggy eminence of considerable girth. The path angles down the left-hand side of

Looking Stead, crosses the marshy ground, then climbs slightly to the right of the first cairned summit before reaching the main summit, which is capped by a cairn and a wind shelter.

▶ There's a difficult crag if you try to go directly north from the summit so first retrace your steps south-westwards to the grassy hollow between the two cairned summits, then descend north-west, mainly on grass. Swing right to the base of those crags to meet the main path, which descends northwards with the crags of **Combe Head** to the right. The path traverses a marshy area and weaves around craggy outcrops to the cairned summit of **Thornythwaite Fell**, with the valley of **Combe Gill** to the right and the fields of Borrowdale ahead.

On the main summit of Glaramara

In mist the next section would present navigational problems as the broad ridge divides at Combe Head.

Views of Borrowdale open up from Thornthwaite Fell

The view down the valley gets more and more impressive, with the little villages of **Seathwaite**, **Seatoller** and **Rosthwaite** coming into view and Skiddaw appearing beyond Derwent Water, which is framed to perfection by the rocky 'Jaws of Borrowdale', Castle Crag and King's How.

The path from Thornythwaite Fell spends most of its time on the east side of the ridge. At NY 247 124 (about 600m from the summit) the path descends sharp right before heading north-east down the west side of the Combe. Not far after some rough slabbed steps take the route down towards the gill, where it passes a waterfall. After going through a gate in the intake wall you enter mixed woodland. The path veers left around the base of the ridge and comes to a gate and stile, beyond which you turn right on an enclosed access lane. This leads you to the Borrowdale road opposite the whitewashed Mountain View cottages.

Cross the road and go straight ahead on an enclosed track to the left of the cottages. Through another gate continue along the left edge of the field before crossing the

STAGE 3A – GREAT LANGDALE TO KESWICK – MOUNTAIN ROUTE

one-arched Folly Bridge. Angle right on a path, which joins a path from **Seatoller**. Turn right along this, staying close to a stone wall on the right into pleasant woodland. When you reach the **River Derwent** the path involves scrambling over some riverside rocks but there are chains provided to ensure your safety.

map continues on page 81

Pass in front of the youth hostel at **Longthwaite** or stop for proper coffee and delicious cakes. A tarred lane takes the route past the car park and over a bridge spanning the river.

Where the lane turns sharp right at Pete Howe, take the path on the left past Foxwood Cottage and through a gate onto a field before following a wall on the right. At the far end of the field the clear path turns right through a gate in the wall and angles right across the next field towards the houses. Beyond a kissing gate it continues behind the houses in a long narrow field.

Through a gate at the end of this turn right along a short stony track leading to a tarred lane, where you turn left between cottages on the outskirts of **Rosthwaite**. Past Nook farm the lane continues to meet the official Cumbria Way at the Flock-in café. Turn right if you are stopping in Rosthwaite, otherwise go left, back to the banks of the Derwent and follow the official way over New Bridge past **Castle Crag** and the **Borrowdale Gates Hotel** (see Stage 3 for full description).

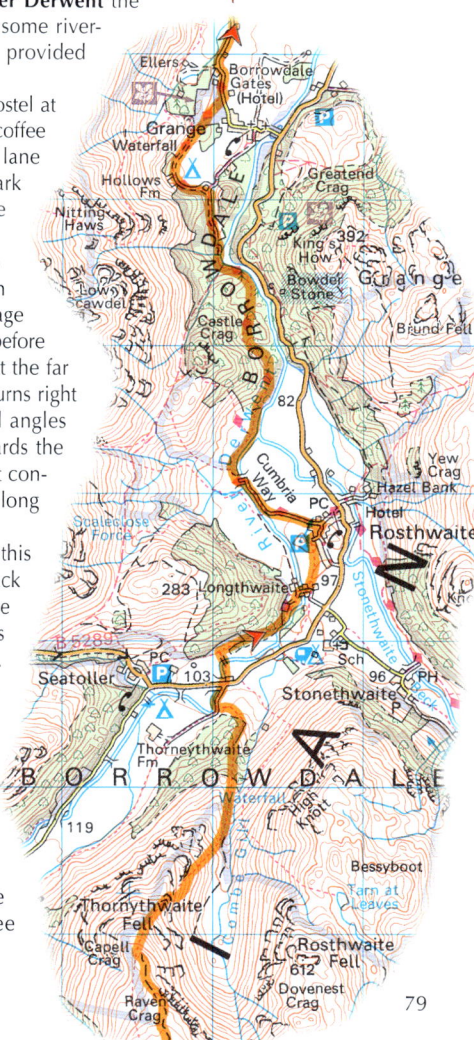

79

Leave the southern shores of Derwent Water beyond the gate at NY 254 186 and follow the right fork path, which soon comes to the engineered path from Lodore. Turn right along this. The path eventually turns right when it meets the Derwent, then crosses on a footbridge. At the far side of the bridge turn right, following the east bank at first. In the next field the path angles half left (south). In the third field it meets a track that follows a small stream out to the road by the Borrowdale Hotel.

Turn left along the road then, after 170m, turn right along a stony track that passes **High Lodore** farm (B&B). This bends left behind the house and narrows into a stony path that climbs beneath and then zigzags up the steep wooded hill slopes of High Lodore.

The gradient eases and the path goes through a gap in a wall (NY 265 183), where you see impressive Shepherd's Crag overlooking **Watendlath Beck** and the top of the **Lodore Falls**. Follow the path towards the beck and its fine cataracts before easing right through Mossmire Coppice.

Crossing Watendlath Beck beyond Mossmire Coppice

STAGE 3A – GREAT LANGDALE TO KESWICK – MOUNTAIN ROUTE

Cross the footbridge over the beck then turn left along the permissive footpath heading northwards to the Watendlath road. Follow it down for about a mile to **Ashness Bridge** and the classic view of Skiddaw across Derwentwater.

Just beyond the bridge fork right along the narrow path to Walla Crag. ▶ Ignore the left fork path seen shortly after the start – that descends into Great Wood. Your path gets to grips with the hillside

Note that the path you're following isn't the footpath marked with green dashes on the OS Explorer but the higher one marked with black dashes.

Ashness Bridge

early on, with a short but easy scramble up rocks. It levels off above **Falcon Crag** and meanders around the hollow of Cat Gill before coming to the wall that straddles the moor. This wall leads the footpath all the way along the ridge to the farmhouse at Rakefoot but to gain the best views go over the stile in the wall, where a path gives access to the rock and heather summit of **Walla Crag**.

The views of **Derwent Water**, **Bassenthwaite**, **Skiddaw** and the **Grasmoor** range of fells are breathtaking, probably the best views on the whole route.

An undulating path continues in fine fashion from the summit cairn of Walla Crag to the rock edge, where it soon comes to the ravine known as **Lady's Rake**.

STAGE 3A – GREAT LANGDALE TO KESWICK – MOUNTAIN ROUTE

BORROWDALE AND DERWENT WATER

Derwent Water and Falcon Crag

Borrowdale was carved by ice from the great glaciers emanating from the snowfields of the Scafells and Great Gable. They scoured out the deep valleys of Langstrath and Seathwaite. When they receded they left four lakes in upper Borrowdale but these disappeared when the river finally broke through the hard volcanic rock forming Grange Fell and Castle Crag, 'the Jaws of Borrowdale'.

The Derwent, whose name means 'river of oaks', meanders north through Borrowdale into Derwent Water before flowing first into Bassenthwaite, then into the sea at Workington. Since Victorian times passenger launches have taken tourists to various landing stages around the lake but in times gone by they would have been transporting Newlands Valley ore for smelting on Rampsholme Island. A lead mine at Brandelhow employed over 70 workers and had a water wheel over 10m in diameter. Derwent Water is home to the vendace, a fresh water whitefish, native only to here, Bassenthwaite Lake and Scotland's Castle Loch and Mill Loch.

There are four main islands on Derwent Water. Derwent Isle near Friar's Crag and the nearest to Keswick is the only one that is inhabited, originally by the monks of Furness Abbey and in the 16th century home to German copper miners from the Mines Royal company. Just to the south lies Lord's Island. Through the undergrowth you may see the crumbled foundations of a 14th-century mansion, once home to Sir Francis Radcliffe, Earl of Derwentwater, who was executed for treason after the Jacobite Rebellion of 1715. Rampsholme Island, opposite Walla Crag, is much smaller. Its name comes from the Old Norse 'Hrafns holmr', which means the island of wild garlic. The larger St Herbert's Island in the middle of the lake has a richer history. It featured as Owl Island in Beatrix Potter's 'The Tale of Squirrel Nutkin' and was used as a hermitage by St Herbert, the seventh-century Northumbrian hermit. He was sent there by his friend and mentor St Cuthbert of Lindisfarne, whom he visited each year for spiritual guidance. It is believed that St Herbert caught and ate fish and grew vegetables from his small cell, the remains of which can still be seen today. Strangely, both Cuthbert and Herbert died on the same day, 20 March AD687. Boat users still land on the islands but they are discouraged from lighting fires or making an overnight stay.

> Lady's Rake is named after **Lady Radcliffe**, wife of the Jacobite supporter, Sir Francis Radcliffe. While the Parliamentary forces were attacking their mansion on Derwent Water's Lord's Island Lady Radcliffe made her escape up the ravine to Walla Crag, it is said, with as many of their treasures as she could muster.

The edge path returns to a gate in the wall and joins the direct path. Leave this after 30m for a faint (at first) grass tack forking right (east). It soon gains confidence and arcs left above the shallow valley of **Brockle Beck**. Now a clear farm track, it descends to cross the beck via a footbridge, which leads to the terminus of a tarred lane.

Turn left along the lane passing the farm at **Rakefoot**. After 200m leave the lane for a path on the left doubling back to a gate before turning right to cross Brockle Beck. At the far side the path turns right again and descends with the beck on the right.

One hundred and fifty metres beyond a radio mast the path veers right, back towards the beck, but don't cross the footbridge over it. Instead turn left down a track, which descends to Spring Farm (café and guesthouse) where you join a tarred lane (Springs Road). This passes houses on the right and fields on the left before coming to Ambleside Road, which takes the route into the centre of **Keswick**.

STAGE 4
Keswick to Caldbeck

Start	Moot Hall
Distance	14½ miles (23km)
Ascent	900m
Approx time	8 hours
Terrain	woodland track around Latrigg followed by easy paths and tracks then one last climb to High Pike (difficult in hill fog)
Maps	OS Explorer OL4 & 5 North Western and North Eastern areas
Supplies	Caldbeck has a shop

Today you leave the Lake District behind. As you round the corner, over the shoulder of Lonscale Fell into the valley of Glenderaterra you can take one last look, one magnificent last look southwards, over the rooftops of Keswick, across the blue expanse of Derwent Water to the craggy peaks of Central Lakeland. But you look forward too: Glenderaterra is a splendid valley dividing Skiddaw and Blencathra and the narrow balcony path that heads north beneath Lonscale Fell's crags will take you to the wild country Back o' Skidda.

If you are confident that the weather will be favourable, you then delve deeper into the hills. The route will take you alongside the infant River Caldew to the summit of the official Cumbria Way at High Pike, where a 360-degree panorama includes Skiddaw, Blencathra, the pale hills of Dumfries and Galloway beyond the Solway Firth and the North Pennines. And laid out beneath your feet is the grassy ridge that eases you down to the fields of Caldbeck. This friendly village waits to replenish your strength for the last section to the city of Carlisle.

▸ Back at the **Moot Hall**, with your back to yesterday's route, take the narrow road to the left of the building and turn first left by the Royal Oak and along **Station Street**. Keep straight on at the crossroads to follow **Station Road**, which passes between the recreation grounds of **Fitz Park**. After the road passes the **Keswick Museum and Art**

See the town map of Keswick at the end of Stage 3.

WALKING THE CUMBRIA WAY

Gallery it curves right. Leave it here for a tarred path on the left passing in front of the Keswick **leisure centre**.

Through the complex you'll come to a mini-roundabout. Go straight across to the other side, where you'll see some steps leading to a path on the left taking the route alongside a roadside hedge with a field on the right. This brings you to another narrow lane and across this the path continues left, again with a hedge keeping you away from the traffic of **Brundholme Road**. The wooded hill of **Latrigg** lies across the fields on the right. The path rejoins the road as it approaches some houses and the route now uses the pavement.

Turn right onto the gravel road known as **Spooneygreen Lane**, which heads for Latrigg. After crossing a bridge over the busy **Keswick bypass** and passing the B&B

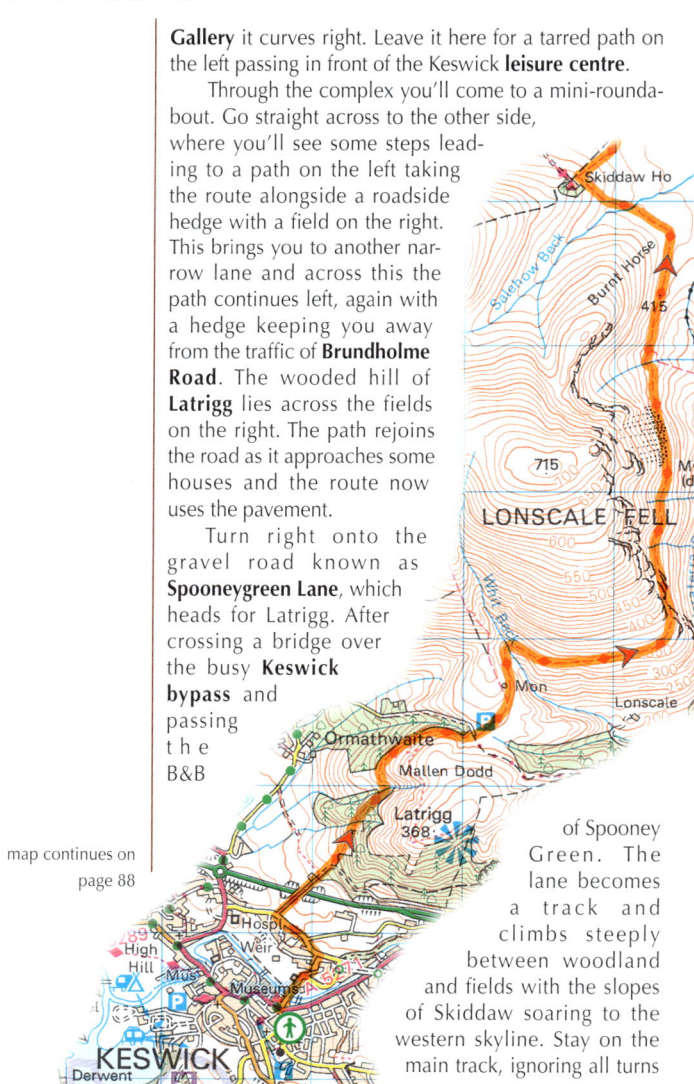

map continues on page 88

of Spooney Green. The lane becomes a track and climbs steeply between woodland and fields with the slopes of Skiddaw soaring to the western skyline. Stay on the main track, ignoring all turns

Skiddaw from below Latrigg

to the right and one left fork to Underscar to arrive at the Skiddaw **car park**. Turn right to the end of the car park, go through the gate and turn left up the wide Skiddaw track.

Through another gate take the right fork path – the left climbs Skiddaw. ▶ This delightful path enters the pretty ravine of **Whit Beck**, where the colours of the waterside larch, the bracken and the heather of the upper slopes make up a fine natural tapestry.

After crossing the beck the track eases across the low slopes of **Lonscale Fell** then turns left into the valley of **Glenderaterra Beck**, which divides the Skiddaw massif from Blencathra.

Stage 4A splits off here.

Look back here for these are your **last views** of the Lakes, from Helvellyn and the Dodds through to the Grasmoor range. Derwent Water is just in view peeping from behind the pastured slopes of Latrigg.

The track undulates as it passes beneath the crags of Lonscale Fell with anonymous heather hills on the horizon. There's a short rocky section but the path is otherwise very easy going. The valley opens out a bit and looking back you can see the impressive pyramidal crags of Lonscale Fell's north-east face. You're joined by a path from the Blencathra side of the valley by a ruined shepherd's hut (sheepfold on the 1:25K Explorer map).

The path rounds the slopes of the **Burnt Horse** ridge and curves left to traverse the wetter, wilder terrain of the Skiddaw Forest. After going over the bridge across **Salehow Beck** follow the path up to the **Skiddaw House** hostel, which is sheltered by wind-warped larch trees. ◄ The way passes in front of the hostel, goes through a gateway in a ruined drystone wall, then turns right on a narrow path alongside that wall. ◄ You cross the infant **River Caldew** on a wooden footbridge in what may seem an insignificant moment. You'll

Stage 4B splits off here.

Current OS maps incorrectly show the route following the near side of the wall.

map continues on page 91

Looking back on Skiddaw House

only be following this stretch for a couple of miles but the Caldew will be your guide for much of the last day into Carlisle.

▶ Further along the path, beneath the heather and stone slopes of **Great Calva**, you'll pass the first of two low circular sheepfolds on the right side of the path. The Cumbria Way continues down the valley and comes across a second perfect circular sheepfold just before crossing **Wiley Gill**, whose coombe separates Great Calva from Knott. The path goes over a footbridge across the gill, climbs to a gate and continues traversing the bracken-clad lower slopes of **Knott**. In the distance lies the more angular and rockier Carrock Fell.

Beyond the crossing of Burdell Gill a track can be seen climbing up Knott's steep slopes. The path that you are following has also now become a wider track and continues parallel to the Caldew with the rugged slopes of **Carrock Fell** making more and more of an impression on the landscape.

Eventually the Way comes to a stone bridge over **Grainsgill Beck** close to the Mosedale road-end. Just beyond the bridge turn left on a mine track signed 'Public

> Looking back from here you'll see Skiddaw's slate slopes rising from behind the now diminutive outlines of Skiddaw House and its larches.

The Lingy Hut

Bridleway to Miller Moss'. This climbs to the spoil heaps and ruined buildings of the Carrock mines.

Just before the crumbling buildings, which are tucked under steep slopes on the far side of the beck, take the upper right fork track. This fades and comes to another track, which descends back to the beck. Ignore the descending track and go straight ahead, on an uncertain path passing a very small cairn. The path gradually becomes more pronounced and comes to the stream of Arm o' Grain by the rubble of some ruined buildings. Over the stream a grass path turns right parallel to the banks. It soon veers away from the stream and climbs north-west as a grassy swathe up the heather slopes of **Great Lingy Hill**.

There's a great retrospective view down the gill to Mosedale, which is flanked by Carrock Fell and the shapely Bowscale Fell.

Stage 4A rejoins here.

As the gradient eases, you pass a large boulder and the Lingy Hut becomes visible on the skyline – the path goes straight to it. ◂ The hut is always open and can offer comfort and shelter should the conditions be less than favourable. ◂

STAGE 4 – KESWICK TO CALDBECK

From the hut the Cumbria Way continues along an easy path that climbs gradually to the Hare Stones, where High Pike, comes into view. Unless you want to climb to Carrock Fell ignore the path on the right and continue on the wide, now stony track for a short way. Ignore the first very faint path on the left as it rounds the summit to the west but if the weather is clear take the second, which climbs to the summit of **High Pike**.

Note If there is hill fog, stay with the main track, which rounds the east side of the fell before winding down to the Sandbed Mine. A left turn on another miners' track will bring you back around the northern slopes of the Pike to the official route at Potts Mine (NY 320 366).

From High Pike's summit the official 'undefined' route descends the north slopes of the fell but a good grass track, not shown on current OS maps, begins from a shelter-cairn just north of the summit. It heads for the distant cottages of Caldbeck at first but then veers slightly left descending towards the right one of two radio masts. The track comes to a crossroads of tracks at NY 318 358. Turn right here and follow the old miners track to the Potts mine.

Here there's another crossroads of tracks and you go straight ahead along

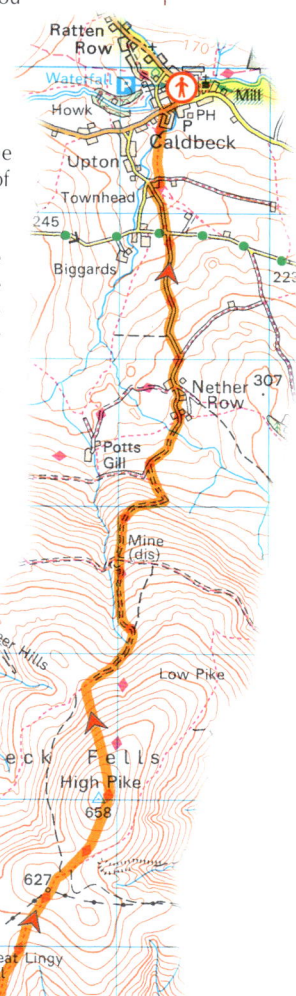

91

Approaching Nether Row from lower northern slopes of High Stile

Stage 4B rejoins here.

a miners' track, which soon zigzags down the mountainside. It joins the grass track of the 'foul weather route' at a wall corner. ◀ A wall on the left, then an old cart track guide the route past the cottages of **Nether Row** to the lane beyond.

Follow the lane through pleasing pastoral countryside to its junction with a road marked on the 1:25K Explorer map as the Street. Go straight ahead on a narrow gravel lane with a 'no vehicle except for access' sign. The lane takes you towards the cottages of **Townhead**. Turn right at a rough grassy triangular green just before the first of them. A fingerpost points to a stile, beyond which you cut diagonally across fields using a metal gate to gain the second field and a stile out to a lane.

On the opposite side of the lane go though a gate and continue on a field path with a wall on the left. A gate leads into woodland, where a narrow path descends to a stream and crosses it on a stone bridge. The hedge-lined path continues to a laneside gate. Through that turn left then right in front of terraced houses to join the main road through **Caldbeck** village, where there's a fine inn, the Oddfellows Arms, a couple of tea shops and a general store.

CALDBECK – A GREAT PLACE TO SPEND HALF A DAY

Caldbeck would be a great place to spend half a day if you can. Named after the river that runs through it, it had its origins in the sixth century when the first church was established. Later monks from Carlisle Priory set up a hospice for travellers. The first part of the current church was established in 1112 and dedicated to the sixth-century preacher of St Kentigern, also known as St Mungo. Further building and renovations took place in the 13th century and 16th centuries. The steeple was added in the seventeenth century with a complete restoration in 1932. At the back of the church by the riverbank lies St Mungo's Well, a spring where early Christians were baptised.

In the churchyard lies a gravestone with elaborate carvings of a hunting horn and whip. This is the resting place of John Peel (1776–1854), a hard-drinking local farmer and huntsman who was immortalised in the words of a song 'Do ye Ken John Peel'. Peel ran a kennel for foxhunting hounds and found time to hunt two or three times a week, mostly for foxes but sometimes for hares. He died after being thrown from his horse. Also buried in the churchyard is Mary Harrison, often referred to as Mary Robinson, the Maid of Buttermere, mentioned in Wordsworth's 'The Prelude'.

St Kentigern's church

Caldbeck's prosperity grew with the mining on the Back o' Skidda fells, in particular on the north side of High Pike, where a band of Borrowdale Volcanic rock separates the Skiddaw slate. The area is rich in lead, copper and barytes. Twenty-three different ores were discovered at the Roughtongill Mine alone. This gave rise to the saying: 'Caldbeck and the Caldbeck Fells are worth all England else'. Mining on a large scale began in the 17th century although it commenced in the 13th century and grew in Elizabethan times when skilled German miners of the Company of the Mines Royal arrived. At Potts Gill/Sandbeds the miners were digging for copper; at Roughtongill it was lead, while at the Carrock Mine it was the rarer wolfram (tungsten).

By the 1850s most of the mines were closed, either because the ores were exhausted or drilling had become uneconomic, but in the 1900s some were utilised for the extraction of barytes, a compound used in drilling fluids for oil extraction and tungsten, which was needed for electric light filaments and to harden steel. Potts Gill/Sandbeds barytes mine finally closed in 1966 while the Carrock tungsten mine closed in 1981.

Walking around the village you'll see many old mills, including Priest's Mill, an old watermill just below the church, which was restored in 1986 and now houses a café and some craft shops. The waterwheel is in full working order. There's a short walk up the Howk at the far end of the village pond, which takes you up a limestone gorge with waterfalls and the impressive ruins of a 19th-century bobbin mill (NY 319397). This once had the country's largest water wheel, measuring 42 feet in diameter. Supplying spinning bobbins for the Lancashire cotton industry, brush and axe handles and soles for clogs the mill once employed over 50 men and boys.

www.caldbeckvillage.co.uk

STAGE 4A
Keswick to Caldbeck – mountain route

Start	Moot Hall
Distance	15¾ miles (25km)
Ascent	1506m
Approx time	9–10 hours
Terrain	Steep mountain path to Skiddaw Low Man followed by easy ridge walk to Bakestall, then undulating moorland to High Pike.
Maps	OS Explorer OL4 & 5 North West and North East
Supplies	Caldbeck has a shop

Now the mountain route is a big one, a bold one, reaching over 3000 feet at Skiddaw. It takes you to the tops of those hills Back o' Skiddaw – Great Calva and Knott are added to High Pike. If the complete mountain section is too much in one go, why not try splitting it by coming down to Skiddaw House for the night (but not without pre-booking)?

Follow Stage 4 from Keswick, around Latrigg, through the Skiddaw car park behind Latrigg. At the junction of tracks beyond a gate in a cross-fence take the left fork, which

Looking from high route on Skiddaw Low Man to the Back o' Skidda valleys of the low route

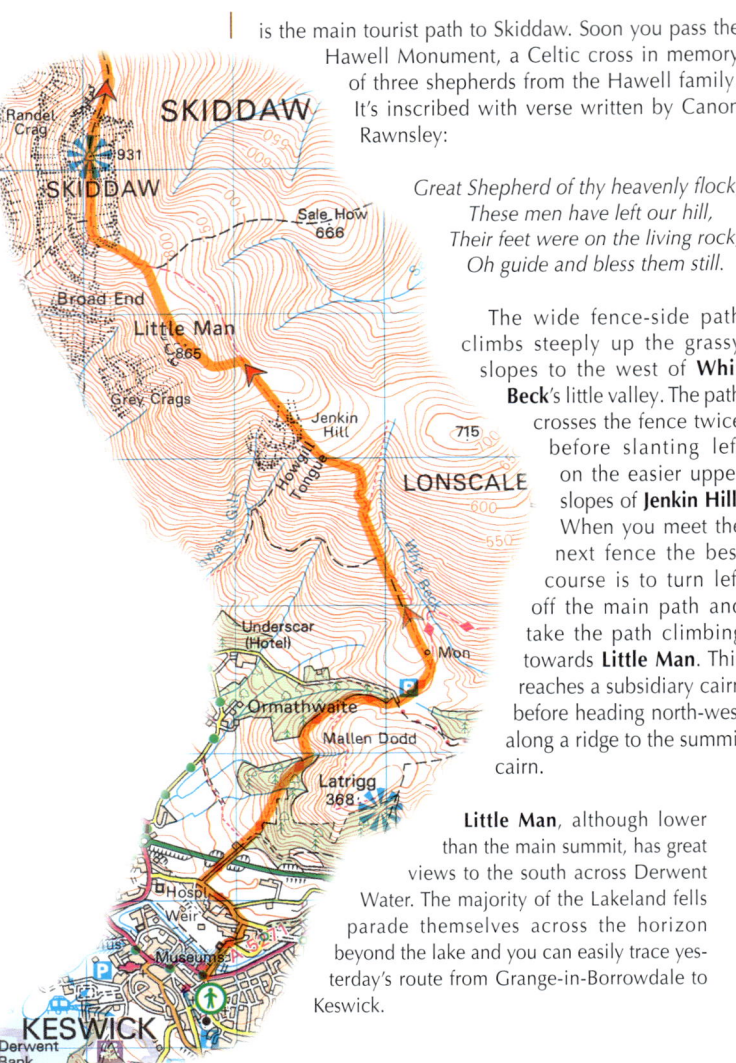

is the main tourist path to Skiddaw. Soon you pass the Hawell Monument, a Celtic cross in memory of three shepherds from the Hawell family. It's inscribed with verse written by Canon Rawnsley:

> *Great Shepherd of thy heavenly flock,*
> *These men have left our hill,*
> *Their feet were on the living rock,*
> *Oh guide and bless them still.*

The wide fence-side path climbs steeply up the grassy slopes to the west of **Whit Beck**'s little valley. The path crosses the fence twice before slanting left on the easier upper slopes of **Jenkin Hill**. When you meet the next fence the best course is to turn left off the main path and take the path climbing towards **Little Man**. This reaches a subsidiary cairn before heading north-west along a ridge to the summit cairn.

Little Man, although lower than the main summit, has great views to the south across Derwent Water. The majority of the Lakeland fells parade themselves across the horizon beyond the lake and you can easily trace yesterday's route from Grange-in-Borrowdale to Keswick.

STAGE 4A – KESWICK TO CALDBECK – MOUNTAIN ROUTE

The path continues by descending to a shallow col beneath Skiddaw's south top. Here the main Skiddaw route joins it from the right. By now the cliffs of **Ullock Pike** are in full view across the scoop of **Southerndale** beck and the sweeping slate-scree sides of **Skiddaw**. The ground beneath your feet gets more slatey with each step. Beyond the cairn on the south top the route climbs to the main summit's trig point and view indicator. ▸

Congratulate yourself! A 3053ft (931m) this is the high point of the whole mountain route.

Continue north along the slate ridge, passing cairns and wind shelters to reach the north top. Beyond this the path descends to join a fence, which will lead you down to **Bakestall**. For views head north at the fence corner to a cairn looking over **Dead Crags** and Birkett Edge.

map continues on page 99

The route now descends north-east after returning to the fence and meets the Skiddaw House track at the top of the **Whitewater Dash** waterfalls. Turn right along it, going through the gate and crossing the footbridge over the beck.

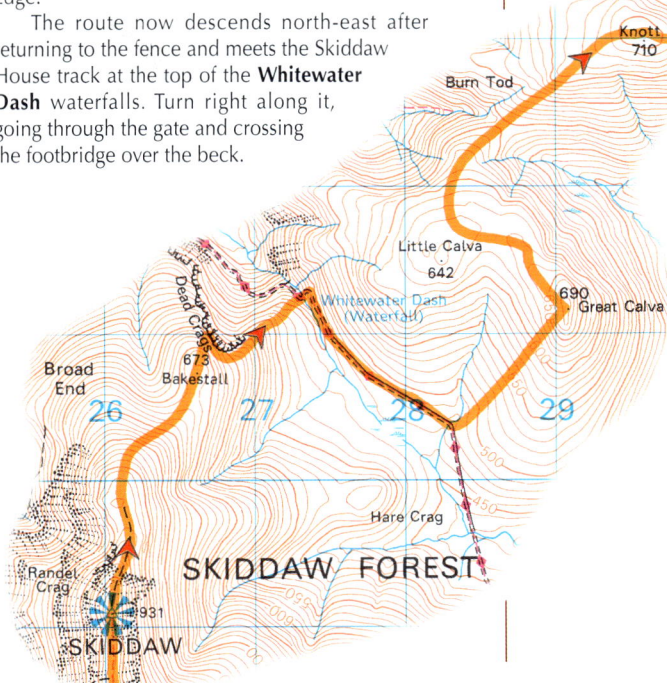

97

The start of path up Great Calva

You could consider a direct **ascent of Little Calva** from here but I wouldn't recommend the route. It is steep, eroded and traverses boggy ground near the summit.

Continue along the track and follow it to the bridge across Dead Beck (NY 283 304, not marked on OS Landranger maps). There's a small tree by the little bridge.

Turn left up a grass track by the beck. This soon becomes a peaty path up the heather slopes of **Great Calva**. In the upper reaches the path becomes steeper and stony. It soon joins a path from Skiddaw House and reaches the first of two cairns. The second marks the summit.

The view back to **Skiddaw** and **Blencathra** is superb and in a gap to the left of the angular escarpment of Lonscale Fell you'll be able to pick out Helvellyn. To the north the wild hills of Caldbeck beckon. Across the deep moorland hollow of Wiley Gill lies

STAGE 4A – KESWICK TO CALDBECK – MOUNTAIN ROUTE

the next, objective, Knott. It's a pale grassy hill with few features from this vantage.

The onward path descends, never far from the ridge fence. It crosses spongy terrain to reach a fence corner at the northern end of Little Calva, Go over a stile here and descend on a narrow path to the col beneath Knott. Now the path climbs up the firm grassy slopes of Knott to reach a small summit cairn.

Looking north you can see **High Pike**, the last summit of the day. It's another pale grassy hill. In between are the marshes of Miller Moss and the heather grounds of Great Lingy Hill. As long as it's not misty you'll be able to pick out Lingy Hut on the right shoulder of the last-mentioned hill. That's where the route heads.

Follow the path from the summit cairn. It goes along the high shoulder of Knott before descending and arcing left to the head of **Grainsgill Beck** and keeping the marshes of **Miller Moss** to the left. Beyond a marshy stream crossing the path makes a beeline across the heather to reach Lingy Hut, where it joins the official route. Follow Stage 4 from here.

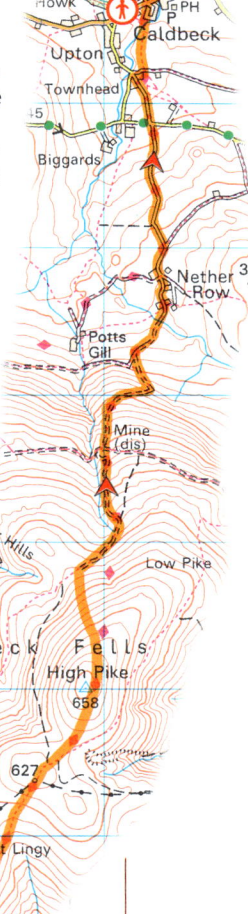

STAGE 4B
Keswick to Caldbeck – foul weather route

Start	Moot Hall
Distance	17¾ miles (28.5km)
Ascent	915m
Approx time	8–9 hours
Terrain	woodland track around Latrigg followed by easy paths and tracks then, from Skiddaw House, good gravel tracks, field paths, and country lanes
Maps	OS Explorer OL4 & 5 North Western and North Eastern areas
Supplies	Caldbeck has a shop

This route shares the initial delights of the views from the Glenderaterra valley and the narrow balcony path beneath Lonscale Fell. But if the cloud is low, there's little point in delving further into the hills from Skiddaw House and there are many delights to be had on this long but easy walk around the north-western edge of the Uldale and Caldbeck fells which meets the main route again just south of Nether Row.

Whitewater Dash Falls

Follow Stage 4 as far as Skiddaw House. After passing in front of Skiddaw House turn left to meet a good stony track by its side gate. This heads north-west, descending slightly at first to cross the **River Caldew** before continuing beneath the heather slopes of **Great Calva**. To the left beyond the sullen expanses of Candleseaves Bog you'll be able to see the steel grey scree slopes of **Skiddaw**. The track meets the mountain route by the crossing of Dead Beck, then traverses more heather slopes.

Follow the track as it descends sharp left to cross Dash Beck just above the **Whitewater Dash** waterfalls, then follows the far bank down into the hollow

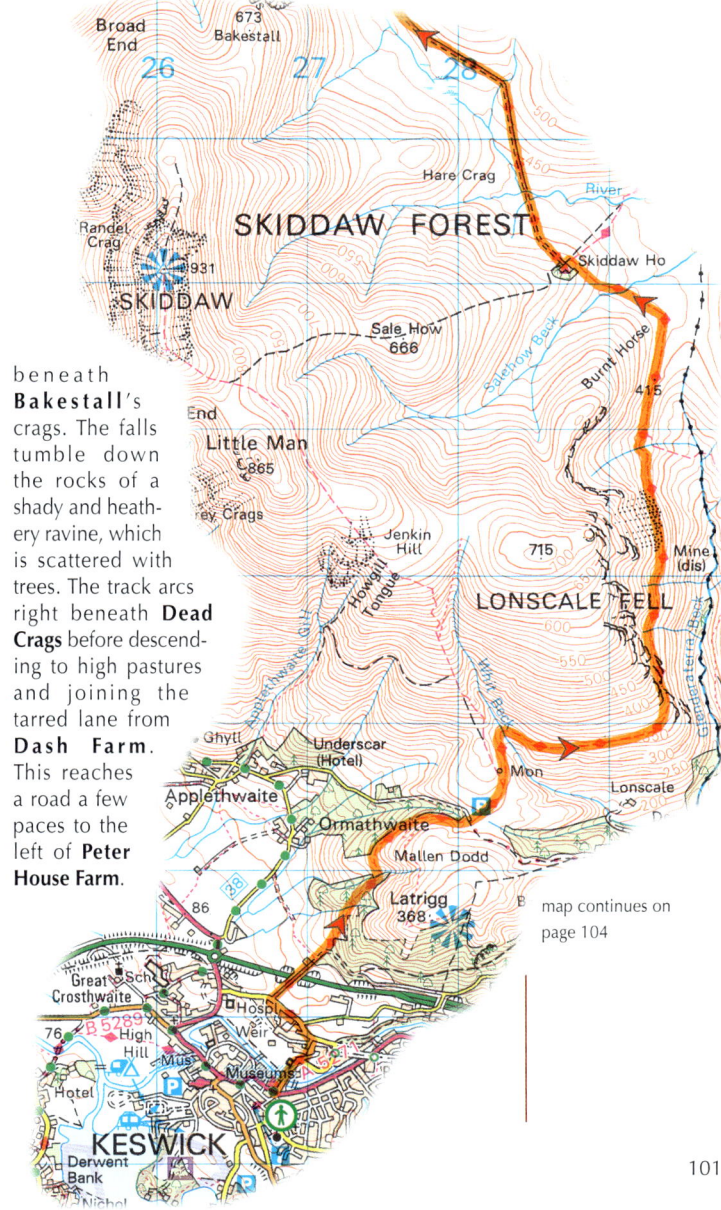

beneath **Bakestall**'s crags. The falls tumble down the rocks of a shady and heathery ravine, which is scattered with trees. The track arcs right beneath **Dead Crags** before descending to high pastures and joining the tarred lane from **Dash Farm**. This reaches a road a few paces to the left of **Peter House Farm**.

map continues on page 104

Whitewater Dash Falls

Cross a stile by a gate on the far side of the road, following the direction indicated by a signpost marked 'public bridleway to Bassenthwaite' – ignore the farm track to the right. At the far side of the field go around the right-hand corner of a small wood to follow a path to a farm gate. Beyond the gate turn right on a path signed to Orthwaite. It follows the field-edge on the right through two fields, passing the whitewashed **Kestrel Lodge**. After crossing a stream the path heads towards Whitefield Wood. Go through a gate on the right and angle down left to meet a track, which leads the route down left into

STAGE 4B – KESWICK TO CALDBECK – FOUL WEATHER ROUTE

the woods. Cross the footbridge over Halls Beck before turning right on a forest track climbing to a tarred lane.

▶ The path climbs with a stream to the right before veering left to reach a gate at the top of the woods. Through this turn right along a stony track. Leave this beyond another gate to head north-east (pathless) over the high left shoulder of the field's summit, then onwards to a gate, beyond which you climb over a ladder stile by a four-way signpost.

Turn right following the route marked CW to Orthwaite. This traverses the gorse-clad slopes above **Little Tarn** before descending to a farm gate and crossing a wide wooden footbridge across a stream. A few paces beyond this go over a step-stile in a fence to the left and continue by the field edge to another gate. Continuing across the next field the way comes to a path junction beyond another gate. Turn right across the field to a roadside stile in the hamlet of **Orthwaite**.

Turn left along the road, passing Orthwaite Hall and climbing high above **Over Water** before descending

On the author's last visit the woods above here were being felled and trees were strewn across the path necessitating detours but this should soon be cleared.

Orthwaite Hall

WALKING THE CUMBRIA WAY

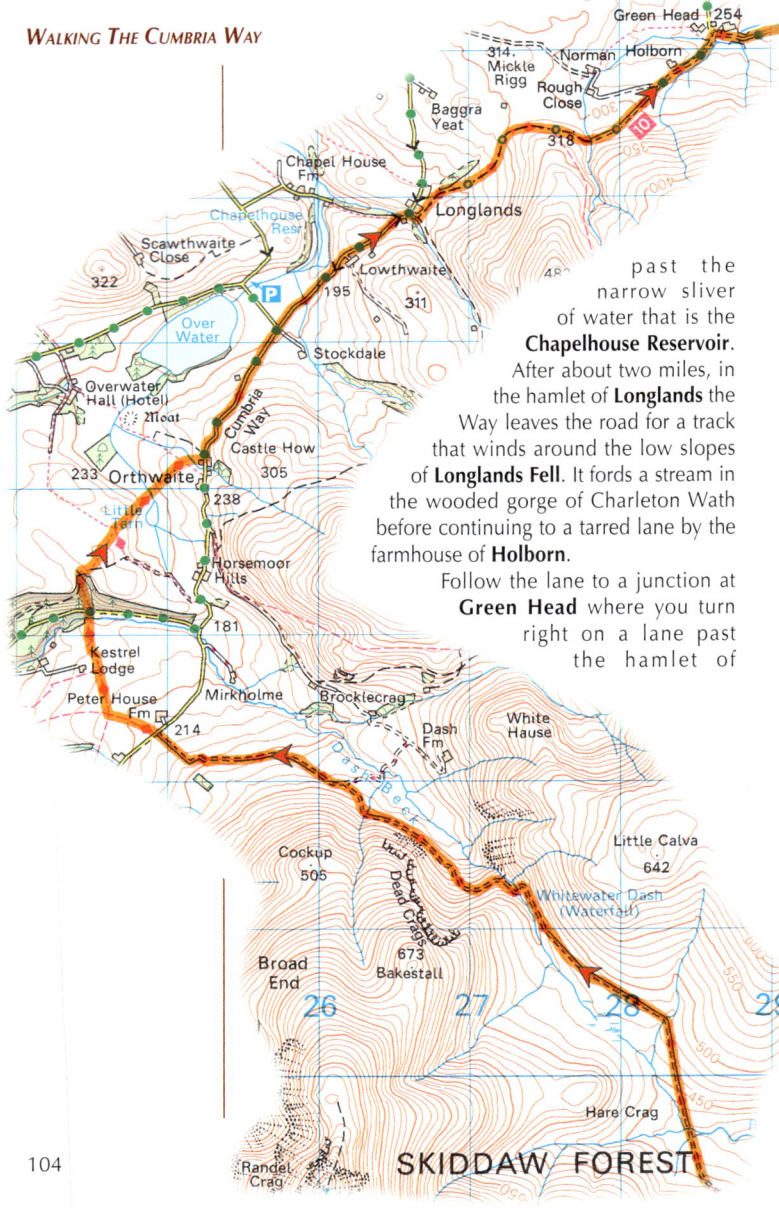

past the narrow sliver of water that is the **Chapelhouse Reservoir**. After about two miles, in the hamlet of **Longlands** the Way leaves the road for a track that winds around the low slopes of **Longlands Fell**. It fords a stream in the wooded gorge of Charleton Wath before continuing to a tarred lane by the farmhouse of **Holborn**.

Follow the lane to a junction at **Green Head** where you turn right on a lane past the hamlet of

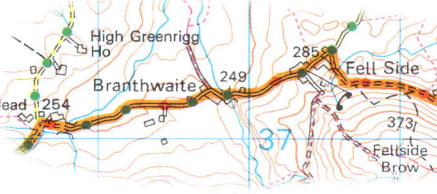
On the foul weather route across the low slopes of High Pike

Branthwaite before climbing to **Fell Side**. Beyond the last building, the Fellside Outdoor Centre, leave the road by turning right along a track that bends left traversing the low slopes of High Pike. The concrete track with a grass island comes to Little Fellside Farm.

Here, current maps show the route as traversing the low edge of the moor to the farm at **Potts Gill**. Have none of it – the line, non-existent on the ground, crosses wet moor and is unpleasant. Instead take the waymarked right fork which traverses the moor a little higher up and meets the high official route at NY 321 372. Turn left along this to **Nether Row**, where you meet the main foul weather route again. Follow Stage 4 from here to **Caldbeck**.

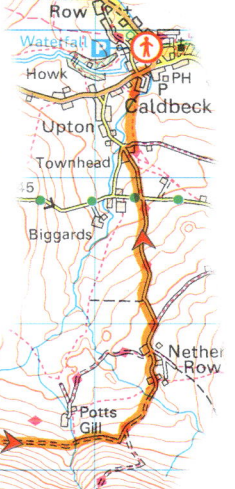

Walking The Cumbria Way

STAGE 5
Caldbeck to Carlisle

Start	Oddfellows Arms
Distance	15½ miles (25km)
Ascent	190m
Approx time	7 hours
Terrain	woodland, riverside and field paths, tarred cycleways and town streets
Maps	OS Explorer OL5 North Eastern area and 315 Carlisle
Supplies	Dalston has a shop; Carlisle has many shops and supermarkets

Today you say goodbye to the Cumbrian Fells and head for the city. As you set off past Caldbeck's church, go over the nearby beck and into the woods of Parson's Park you might feel like the best is behind you, and maybe it is… there again maybe it's not.

This quiet part of Cumbria has its charms and its little surprises. As you climb through the woods there are fine retrospective views across the pretty undulating pastures and farmhouses of Caldbeck and its satellite villages to High Pike and the Back o' Skidda and soon the route reacquaints itself with the Caldew, which you first met near Skiddaw House. This river will lead you for much of the way through pleasant countryside to Carlisle. On the way you'll see several historic bridges and an ancient ecclesiastical castle.

It would be a shame to get the first train out of Carlisle when you finish your walk. This is a fine city and should not be missed. You'll need half a day to explore the cathedral quarter and the castle, then there's the Tullie House Museum, where you can learn more about the history of the city, including its Roman past.

With your back to the **Oddfellows Arms** walk down the main street past the stores before turning left down a surfaced path on the nearside of the **church**. After going over a stone bridge over Cald Beck turn right on a lane (Friar's Row) past some housing and parallel to the river.

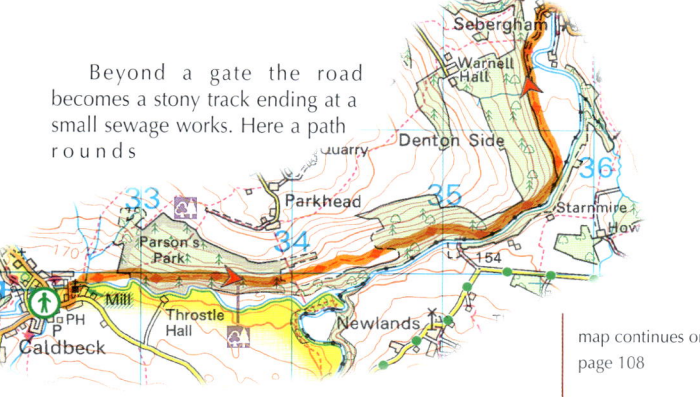

Beyond a gate the road becomes a stony track ending at a small sewage works. Here a path rounds

map continues on page 108

the works to the right, continues by the beck and enters the woodland of **Parson's Park**. Follow the stony Cumbria Way path as it veers left uphill and then returns to running parallel to the beck.

There are **fine views** back over immature trees to yesterday's walk, with whitewashed farmhouses and trees scattered across the undulating and very green pastures of Caldbeck, all this backed up by High Pike and the Caldbeck Fells.

Through a gate the route enters sloping fields recently planted (2021) with oak and birch trees. Go straight ahead on a grassy ride, ignoring paths descending right.

If you look down right you'll see a tree-lined river that has meandered through the pastures to the south to join Cald Beck. It is our old friend the **River Caldew**, which we last met on the route between Skiddaw House and the Carrock mines area. You'll see a lot more of the Caldew on the journey to Carlisle.

As you come to the far end of the new planation climb slightly left to the bridleway gate – ignore the farm gate below right. In the next field follow the lower edge of

WALKING THE CUMBRIA WAY

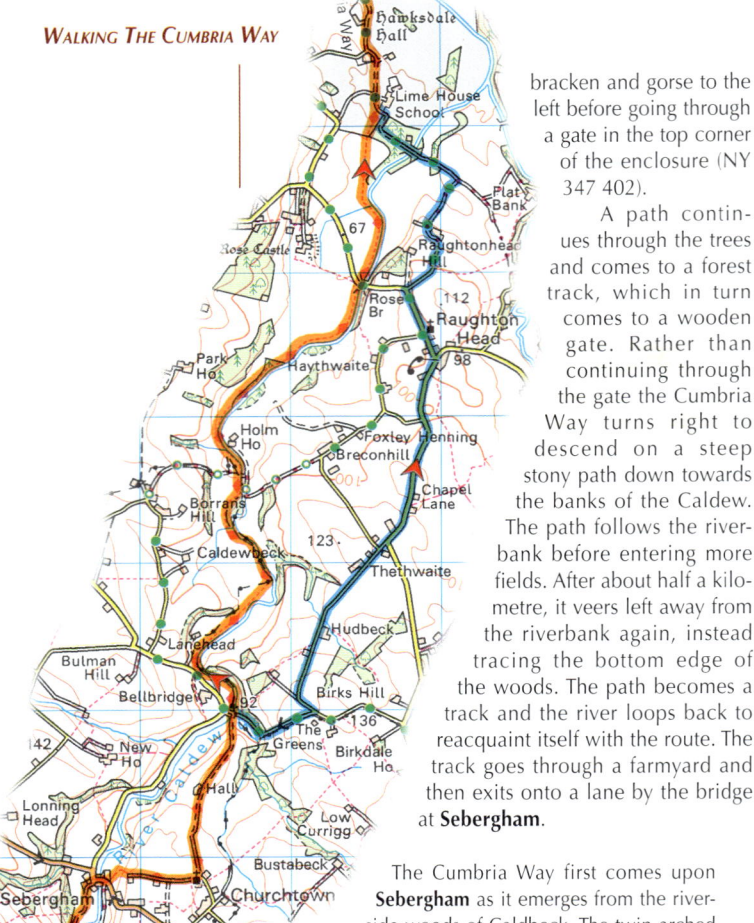

map continues on page 113

bracken and gorse to the left before going through a gate in the top corner of the enclosure (NY 347 402).

A path continues through the trees and comes to a forest track, which in turn comes to a wooden gate. Rather than continuing through the gate the Cumbria Way turns right to descend on a steep stony path down towards the banks of the Caldew. The path follows the riverbank before entering more fields. After about half a kilometre, it veers left away from the riverbank again, instead tracing the bottom edge of the woods. The path becomes a track and the river loops back to reacquaint itself with the route. The track goes through a farmyard and then exits onto a lane by the bridge at **Sebergham**.

The Cumbria Way first comes upon **Sebergham** as it emerges from the riverside woods of Caldbeck. The twin-arched sandstone bridge spanning the River Caldew was built in 1689. Sited among fields above the river and at the end of a long narrow lane, Sebergham's square-towered church first appears through the trees, its old red sandstone walls crusted with lichen. Its peaceful setting gives a clue to its origins, for in the 12th century a hermit, William de

Approaching the church at Sebergham seen through the trees

la Wastell, set up home here. This saintly man also set up the first church on the site. The church you see today has medieval roots but was substantially restored in the 1820s. At this time the tower was added. The four lancet windows date from the 13th century.

▶ Go over the bridge and round the first bend. Just beyond a stone cottage turn left through a gate and follow a path signed as a bridleway to Sedbergham church. This soon takes a muddy and steep course up to the right to a small gate. Through this you pass a whitewashed cottage, then a substantial brick house, where a lane takes the route to the **church**.

Turn left at the church through a wide gate and follow the bridleway track signed to Bell Bridge. This passes in front of Sebergham Hall and continues across fields to the road. Turn left over the one-arched stone-built Bell Bridge.

The old 18th-century Bell Bridge collapsed in January 2016 after being badly damaged by the floods of December 2015, but was rebuilt as a modern sandstone bridge and completed in December 2017.

By the river Caldew near Bog Bridge

> If the meadows are flooded here, take the 'Flood route via Lime House School' described on p112.

◀ From the far side of the Bell Bridge go over a stile and down some steep steps to riverside meadows. The path simply follows the tree-lined riverbank as it meanders through meadowland, then fields of crops, going through gates at the field edges en route. At one point the path comes a short way left, away from the river, to cross a stream on a little footbridge but immediately returns to the Caldew and follows it to Bog Bridge. Do not cross this bridge, but continue by the riverbank on a path signed to Rose Bridge.

The Way soon passes through a short stretch of mixed woodland that is carpeted with wild garlic in spring and summer and then continues across the fields of the **Rose Castle** estate to **Rose Bridge**.

Do not cross Rose Bridge but go through the kissing gate opposite, and continue on a riverside path signed to Holm Hill.

The river meanders left and the path goes through a gate and over a little footbridge. Now the river bends sharp

STAGE 5 – CALDBECK TO CARLISLE

ROSE CASTLE

Were it not for its castellated red sandstone pele tower you could be forgiven for thinking Rose Castle – first seen across expansive fields to the west of the River Caldew – was a highbrow public school. In fact, the castle was first built for Bishop Walter Mauclerc after land was gifted to the church by Henry II in 1230 and has been the palace of the Bishops of Carlisle ever since. It is not open to the public but you can divert from the route along a path from Rose Bridge to get a closer look.

In the early days the buildings would have been made of wood but these were badly battered in border raids. The stone castle that followed was fortified and built around four sides of a central courtyard. In the 15th centuries towers were added. The castle suffered again during the Civil War and in 1648 the departing Parliamentary troops burnt the place down. Once again restored in the 1760s it was visited by Wordsworth and Coleridge in 1803. Coleridge wrote: 'We are delighted with Rose Castle, the thickset green fence to the garden, the two walls, the lower making a terrace / the House, the Orchard crowding round it – The Chestnuts – the masses of Ivy over the gateway, from one great root – all, all perfect ... Cottage Comfort & ancestral Dignity!'

Much of the castle seen today belongs to the early 19th century, a product of yet further restoration work undertaken for Bishop Percy by Thomas Rickman and Anthony Salvin.

Bell Bridge, one of the many Caldew bridges seen on the last day

right. At the crown in this bend and by a large sandy river island the path heads north, away from the river.

Cross a stile and footbridge and then climb to a distant gate. Through this follow the narrow path ahead to the left edge of Willowclose Wood. Beyond another gate turn left on a track signed 'Holm Hill and Dalston'. The track comes to the **Lime House School** access road at a left hand bend. Look back to see the school's imposing buildings.

Flood Route via Lime House School

Occasionally the meadows between Bell Bridge and Lime House School flood. If this is the case don't descend from Bell Bridge to the riverside meadows on the other side but turn right at the end of the track just before the bridge, then left at the next junction, signed Hudbeck and Raughtonbeck. After about 1½ miles, fork left at a road junction to reach **Raughton Head**. Turn left (signed Welton, Dalston and Carlisle) and pass the **church** where you keep straight on.

Where the road turns left turn right onto the lane signed to **Raughtonhead Hill**, a brick-built farmhouse. The

STAGE 5 – CALDBECK TO CARLISLE

road bends left and then terminates beyond another brick cottage. Continue on a signed and enclosed bridleway track before turning right at a Y junction, then left at a T junction of tracks. Ignore a right fork track into a field but carry straight on across the River Caldew at Highwath Bridge to enter Willowclose Wood. At the far end of this patch of mixed woodland the track bends right towards the buildings of **Lime House School**, then turns left to join the Cumbria Way.

The onward route begins across the track and continues north as a field path, eventually passing between Holmhill Farm (left) and a large modern house (right).

Beyond these a track climbs to a lane corner. Turn right along the lane to **Hawksdale Hall**. Here the lane ends and a track on the right continues across cow pastures before bending left towards some houses. Beyond a gate the track becomes a lane passing in front of the houses and out onto the Dalston Road.

Turn right down the road and take the right fork by the **Bridge End Inn** to cross the Caldew on Hawksdale Bridge. Turn right at the far side of the bridge along a path signed to

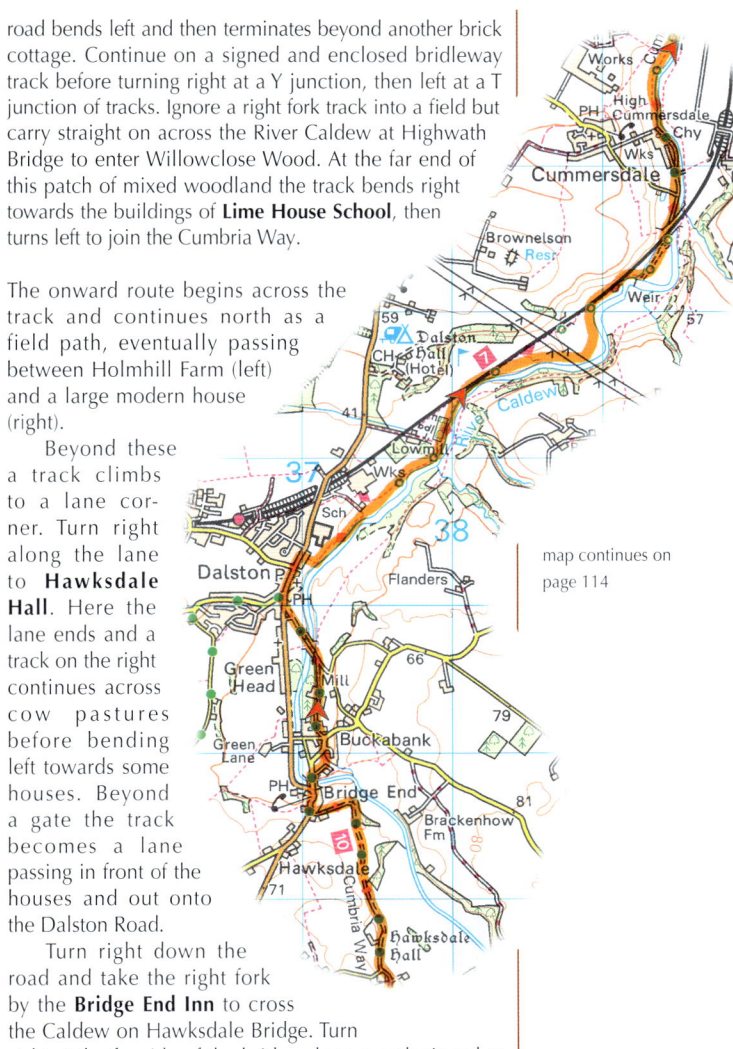

map continues on page 114

113

The River Caldew at Dalston

the Raughton Road. After following the river to a farm by a weir go though double gates on the left and immediately through another set of gates, keeping the farmhouse to the left. Where the farm track turns left beyond the house go through a gate ahead and across a field to the Raughton Road.

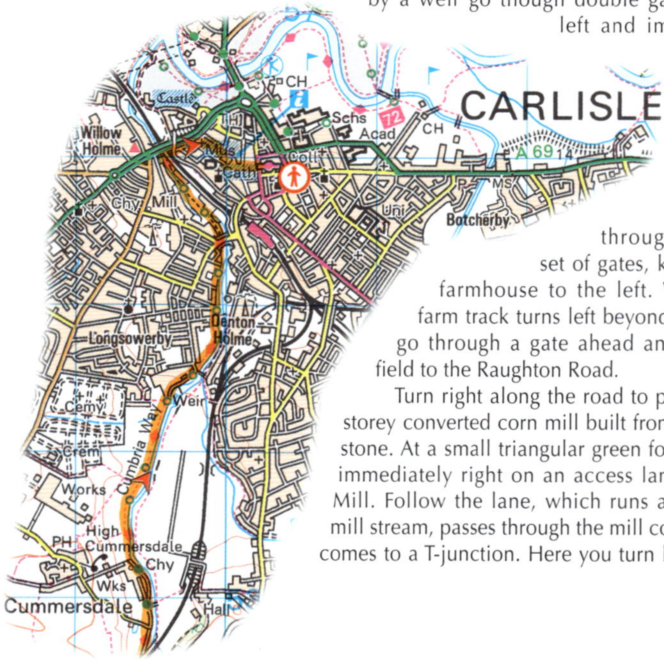

Turn right along the road to pass a three storey converted corn mill built from red sandstone. At a small triangular green fork left then immediately right on an access lane to Ellers Mill. Follow the lane, which runs alongside a mill stream, passes through the mill complex and comes to a T-junction. Here you turn left along a tarred track to cross the White Bridge over the Caldew before coming out to the road just south of **Dalston**'s village centre.

> You may have noticed that there's a route into Carlisle from here using paths on the **east side** of the river. Don't even think about it; the paths are slimy with mud for long stretches in woodland and you'll end up in the city caked with that mud and a couple of hours later than you expected.

Turn right along the main road through the village, then right again beyond the school on a signed tarred cycleway, which soon turns left roughly following the Caldew.

The best route often leaves it to follow the riverbank. Although it's longer to do this it will come as welcome break between the tarmac you've walked so far and will have to walk later. The first of these begins at NY 374 506, avoiding the huge Nestlé factory. Two more riverside paths avoid the dull tarmac route that traces the railway track of the Dalston line.

Beyond the third and final detour the cycleway passes beneath a railway bridge and comes to a lane end near **Cummersdale**. Go straight ahead here on a short stretch of tarred lane to some factory gates, to the right of which a narrower cycleway continues with the huge mill factory to the left. ▶

A short way beyond the far end of the factory (NY 394 533) a waymarker highlights another detour to the right of the cycleway. The path passes through a short stretch of woodland before entering fields. By now the houses of Carlisle's outskirts appear to the right across fields on the far side of the river.

As the path approaches the houses of **Denton Holme** ignore paths to the left. At a three-way signpost go right along path signed Denton Holme, between a converted mill and the river, passing the Holme Head **weir** and coming to a modern footbridge over the river (which you don't cross).

The Carlisle Southern Link Road is being built across the line of the Cumbria Way at Cummersdale, which may impact the Caldew Cycleway. Check with the Dalston Parish Council website before setting out (www.dalston.org.uk). The construction is due to be completed by summer 2025.

Continue on the tarred cycleway past the houses of Denton Holme. You'll come across floodgates built after the great Carlisle floods of 2005. Follow the signed cycleway through Carlisle passing in front of the modern brick-built flats of McIlmoyle Way. Beyond a left-hand bend and past the floodgates at the end of Lime Street the route follows the line of a dismantled railway, which goes under Nelson (road) Bridge and then crosses the river on a wide bridge.

Turn right 260m beyond the bridge to pass between industrial units, then turn left along Viaduct Estate Road, which runs alongside the main railway line. Follow this up to Bridge Street where you turn right. ◀ Pass under the archway and turn right on historic Abbey Street. Through a gatehouse in the old city walls you pass through the magnificent Cathedral Quarter. Beyond the quarter turn right along Castle Street to reach the Market Cross – the official end of the Cumbria Way.

If you want to visit the castle you can climb the steps to and cross the Millennium Footbridge over the busy A595.

CARLISLE

Carlisle Castle

Carlisle was part of an area ruled by the Celtic Carvetii tribe. Its name comes from the Celtic god, Lugh, which in turn evolved into Caer Luel (the fortress of Lugh) then Carlisle. The Romans overran the area in AD73 and built their fort, Luguvalium, on a site between the castle and the Abbey Gate. This became an important settlement just behind Hadrian's Wall.

It is believed that after the Roman occupation ended in around AD400 Carlisle joined the Brythonic (Celtic) kingdom of Rheged. At the time of the Norman Conquest of 1066 the area had become part of Scotland but William Rufus (William II) drove the Scots out before establishing Carlisle Castle in 1093. The old timber castle was replaced in 1112 by the great sandstone fortress you see today and the construction included city walls

STAGE 5 – CALDBECK TO CARLISLE

with three gates; Botcher (English) Gate, Scotch Gate and Caldew (Irish) Gate.

In 1122, during the reign of Henry I, the Augustinian canons founded the Priory of St Mary. Eleven years later the king established the Diocese of Carlisle and the priory church became the cathedral. In 1233 Dominican (Blackfriar) and Franciscan (Greyfriar) friaries were also established close to the cathedral. These were 'dissolved' in 1536 by Henry VIII. The English Civil War was a miserable time of siege and starvation for the prosperous city and it surrendered to the Parliamentarians in 1645. The conquering army demolished much of the cathedral's long west nave, its cloisters and chapter house, using the stone to reinforce Carlisle Castle. After the restoration of the monarchy in 1660 there was a period of rebuilding in the city with a new town hall, the one you see today in Market Square, Tullie House, now a museum, and many grand early Georgian-style houses.

Turmoil returned again to the city in the form of the Jacobite Rebellion. The Young Pretender, Bonnie Prince Charlie, took the city in 1745 and left a garrison force of 400 there before heading south to London to fight for the English throne. In the end, the prince turned back at Derby and was forced to retreat by the Duke of Cumberland, George II's son, who retook the city with ease. He captured many of the Jacobite rebels and imprisoned them in the castle's dungeons before defeating the rebel army at Culloden.

Today Carlisle is a prosperous city with much to offer the tourist, who can view the castle (open March: at weekends 10am–4pm, Apr–Sept: 10am–6pm, Oct–Nov: 10am–5pm; Tel: 01228 591922; www.english-heritage.org.uk), check out Cumbrian history at the Tullie House Museum (open Apr–Oct: Mon–Sat 10am–5pm, Sun 11am–5pm, Nov–Mar: Mon–Sat 10am–4pm, Sun 12–4pm; Tel: 01228 618718; enquiries@tulliehouse.co.uk; www.tulliehouse.co.uk) or best of all wander through the cathedral quarter (cathedral open

The great sandstone cathedral

WALKING THE CUMBRIA WAY

Mon–Sat 7.30am–6.15pm, Sun 7.30am–5pm). The Guildhall Museum in Green Market is a museum of civic history housed in Carlisle's only medieval house (open July–early Oct: 12–4pm).

www.discovercarlisle.co.uk

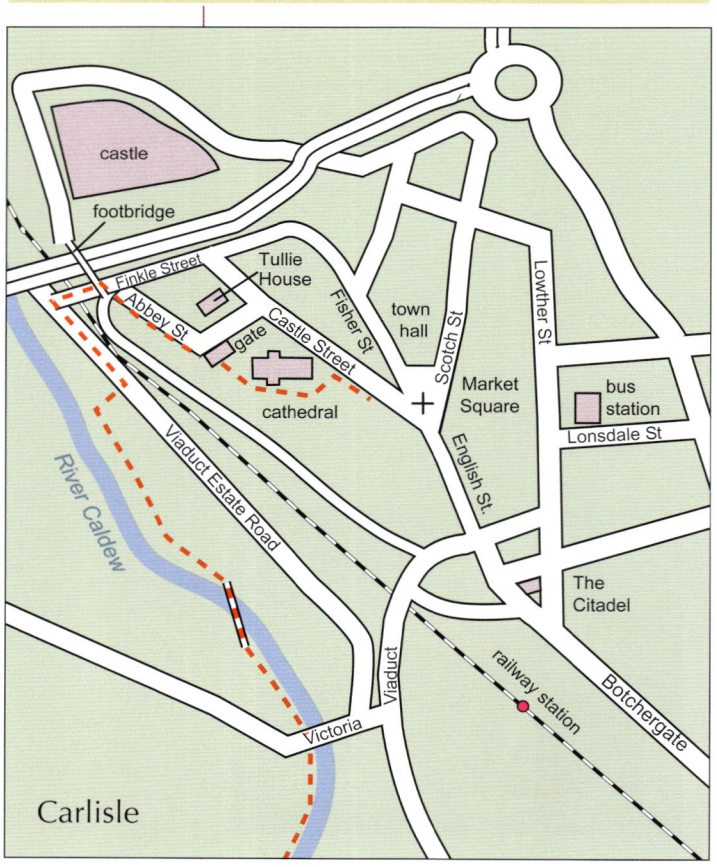

APPENDIX A
Route summary table

Official route

Stage	Distance	Ascent	Approx time	Page no
1 Ulverston to Coniston	15½ miles (25km)	615m	7–8hrs	30
2 Coniston to Great Langdale	11¾ miles (19km)	550m	5–6hrs	44
3 Great Langdale to Keswick	16 miles (25.5km)	645m	8–9hrs	61
4 Keswick to Caldbeck	14½ miles (23km) ; foul weather: 17¾ miles (28.5km)	900m; foul weather: 915m	8hrs; foul weather: 8–9hrs	85
5 Caldbeck to Carlisle	15½ miles (25km)	190m	7hrs	106

Mountain route

Stage	Distance	Ascent	Approx time	Page no
1 Ulverston to Torver	12 miles (19km)	615m	6–7hrs	30
2A Torver to Great Langdale	15½ miles (25km)	1130m	8–9hrs	55
3A Great Langdale to Keswick	17½ miles (28km)	1430m	9–10hrs	74
4A Keswick to Caldbeck	15¾ miles (25km)	1506m	9–10hrs	95
5 Caldbeck to Carlisle	15½ miles (25km)	190m	7hrs	106

Derwent Water at dusk (Stage 3)

APPENDIX B
Facilities table

	Distance	Cumulative distance	Facilities
Official route			
Ulverston	0	0	campsite, B&Bs, hotel, buses, trains
Lowick Bridge (1 mile off route)	7½ miles (12km)	7½ miles (12km)	Red Lion Inn, buses
Cockenskell Farm	2 miles (3km)	9½ miles (15km)	B&B at farm, book well in advance
Torver (1½ miles off main route)	2½ miles (4km)	12 miles (19km)	campsites, inn, shop, buses
Coniston Hall	2½ miles (4km)	14½ miles (23km)	campsite
Coniston	1 mile (1.5km)	15½ miles (25km)	inns, B&Bs, shops, cafes, youth hostels (2), buses
High Park	4¾ miles (7.5km)	20¼ miles (32.5km)	B&B, cafe
Elterwater Park	1 mile (1.5km)	21¼ miles (34km)	B&B
Skelwith Bridge	1 mile (1.5km)	22¼ miles (35.5km)	hotel, pub, café, buses,
Elterwater	1½ miles (2.5km)	23¾ miles (38km)	inn, café, buses,
Chapel Stile	1 mile (1.5km)	24¾ miles (39.5km)	pub, shop, buses,

	Distance	Cumulative distance	Facilities
Dungeon Ghyll	2½ miles (4km)	27¼ miles (43.5km)	inns, pub/café, campsite, buses
Stonethwaite	6¾ miles (11km)	34 miles (54.5km)	inn, campsite
Rosthwaite	1 mile (1.5km)	35 miles (56km)	B&B, inn, hotel, youth hostel, café, buses
Grange	2½ miles (4km)	37½ miles (60km)	B&B, hotel, campsite, buses
Portinscale	4½ miles (7km)	42 miles (67km)	hotel, buses
Keswick	1¼ miles (2km)	43¼ miles (69km)	inns, B&Bs, cafes, shops, youth hostel, buses
Skiddaw House	5½ miles (9km)	48¾ miles (78km)	youth hostel, camping
Bassenthwaite (off route)	4¾ miles (7.5km)	53½ miles (85.5km)	pub, B&Bs, buses
Caldbeck	4¼ miles (7km)	57¾ miles (92.5km)	inn, B&B, campsite, shop, café, buses
Dalston	11 mile (17.5km)	68¾ miles (110km)	B&B, café, shops, buses, trains
Carlisle	4½ miles (7km)	73¼ miles (117km)	hotels, B&Bs, shops, cafes, youth hostel, buses, trains

Mountain route

	Distance	Cumulative distance	Facilities
Ulverston	0	0	campsite, B&Bs, hotel, buses, trains
Lowick Bridge (1 mile off route)	7½ miles (12km)	7½ miles (12km)	inn, buses

Appendix B – Facilities table

	Distance	Cumulative distance	Facilities
Cockenskell Farm	2 miles (3km)	9½ miles (15km)	B&B at farm book well in advance
Torver	2½ miles (4km)	12 miles (19km)	campsites, inns, shops, buses
Little Langdale	10¾ miles (17km)	22¾ miles (36.5km)	inn
Elterwater	1¼ miles (2km)	24 miles (38.5km)	inn, café, buses
Chapel Stile	1 mile (1.5km)	25 miles (40km)	inn, shop, buses
Dungeon Ghyll	2½ miles (4km)	27½ miles (44km)	inns, pub/café, campsite, buses
Longthwaite	7½ miles (12km)	35 miles (56km)	youth hostel
Rosthwaite	1 mile (1.5km)	36 miles (57.5km)	B&B, inn, hotel, youth hostel, café, buses
Lodore	4¼ miles (7km)	40¼ miles (64.5km)	hotel, B&B, buses
Castlerigg	3¾ miles (6km)	44 miles (70.5km)	inn, campsites
Keswick	1¼ miles (2km)	45¼ miles (72.5km)	inns, B&Bs, cafes, shops, youth hostel, buses
Skiddaw House	7¾ miles (12.5km)	53 miles (85km)	youth hostel (1 mile off route)
Caldbeck	8 miles (13km)	61 miles (97.5km)	inn, B&B, campsite, shop, café, bus
Dalston	11 mile (17.5km)	72 miles (115km)	B&B, café, shops, buses, trains
Carlisle	4½ miles (7km)	76½ miles (122km)	hotels, B&Bs, shops, cafes, youth hostel, buses, trains

Relaxing at the Old Dungeon Ghyll Hotel (Stage 2)

APPENDIX D
Useful contacts

Tourist Information Centres
Ulverston
Coronation Hall
County Square
Tel 01229 587120
info@visitulverston.com

Coniston
Ruskin Ave
Tel 015394 41533
mail@conistontic.org

Ambleside (for Great Langdale)
Central Buildings
Market Cross
Tel 015394 32729
tic@thehubofambleside.com

Keswick (for Borrowdale)
Moot Hall
Market Square
Tel 0845 9010845
keswicktic@lakedistrict.gov.uk

Carlisle (for Caldbeck northwards)
Old Town Hall
CA3 8J
Tel 01228 625600
etourism@carlisle.gov.uk

Accommodation websites
National Trust campsites and B&Bs
www.nationaltrust.org.uk/holidays

Booking.com
www.booking.com

Laterooms.com
www.laterooms.com

Camping
www.ukcampsite.co.uk

Youth Hostel Association
www.yha.org.uk

Lakeland Camping Barns
www.lakelandcampingbarns.co.uk

Public transport between stages
By train
www.thetrainline.com

Dalston near the end of the walk is on the Cumbria Coastal Line with links to both Ulverston and Carlisle.

By bus
For the latest information on buses see www.cumbria.gov.uk. Select 'find a bus timetable' from the 'roads and travel' drop-down menu.

Ulverston to Coniston: The X12 (Blueworks Private Hire) links the two places and calls at Torver and Sunnybank. For those abandoning the Way the 505 runs from Coniston to Ambleside where you can pick up the 555 linking Lancaster (West Coast Main Line) and Keswick.

Coniston to Dungeon Ghyll: The 505 to Ambleside links with the 516 to Dungeon Ghyll, which stops at Skelwith Bridge, Elterwater and Chapel Stile en route.

Dungeon Ghyll to Keswick: The 78 links Seatoller, Rosthwaite with Keswick. The 77 links Grange and Portinscale with Keswick.

Keswick to Caldbeck: The limited 73 service around the Skiddaw/Blencathra massif to Caldbeck and onwards to

Hollows Farm
nr Grange
NY 284 170
Tel 017687 77298
www.hollowsfarm.co.uk

Castlerigg Hall (above Keswick, ideal for mountain route via Walla Crag)
NY 281 226
Tel 017687 74499
www.castlerigg.co.uk
No advance bookings for tents

Castlerigg Farm (above Keswick, ideal for mountain route via Walla Crag)
NY 283 224
Tel 017687 72479
www.castleriggfarm.com
No advance bookings for tents

Hostels
YHA Borrowdale
Longthwaite
Rosthwaite
NY 255 142
Tel 0345 371 9624
Open summer and selected weekends

YHA Keswick
Station Road
Tel: 0345 371 9746
Open all year

Dinah Hoggus Camping Barn
Stonecroft
Borrowdale
NY 259 150
Tel 017687 77689
www.lakelandcampingbarns.co.uk
2 nights only on Fri and Sat

Derwentwater Independent Hostel
Borrowdale (east side of Derwent Water)
NY 268 200
Tel 017687 77246
contact@derwentwater.org
http://derwentwater.org

Stage 4/4A/4B
Hotels, inns and B&Bs
The Oddfellows Arms
Caldbeck
Tel 016974 78227
www.oddfellows-caldbeck.co.uk

There are several B&Bs in Caldbeck. For up-to-date information visit www.caldbeckvillage.co.uk.

Campsites
Throstle Hall Caravan Park
NY 331 398 (to the east of Caldbeck)
Tel 016974 78618, mounsey.r4@btinternet.com
Cumbria Way walkers welcome for one night (otherwise only caravans)

Caldbeck Camping
www.caldbeckcamping.co.uk
Right on Cumbria Way near the entrance to Parsons Park
Tel 01697 478367

Hostels
Hudscales Camping Barn, Hesket Newmarket (a mile east of Nether Row)
NY 332 376
Tel 016974 78637 (booking office)
www.lakelandcampingbarns.co.uk

Stage 5
Hotels, inns and B&Bs
Being a city Carlisle has hotels and B&Bs of all types and sizes. Tourist Information Centre: Tel 01228 598596
www.discovercarlisle.co.uk

Hostels
Carlisle City Hostel
Abbey Street, Carlisle
Tel: 07914 720821
http://carlislecityhostel.com/wp

Skelwith Bridge Hotel
Tel 015394 32115
www.skelwithbridgehotel.co.uk

Britannia Hotel
Elterwater
Tel 015394 37210
http://thebritanniainn.com

New Dungeon Ghyll Hotel
Tel 015394 37213
www.dungeon-ghyll.co.uk

Old Dungeon Ghyll Hotel
Tel 015394 37272
www.odg.co.uk

Campsites
Baysbrown Farm
Chapel Stile
Great Langdale
NY 356 053 (on the route)
No advance bookings
www.baysbrownfarmcampsite.co.uk

National Trust Campsite
Old Langdale Campsite
Great Langdale
NY 287 058
No advance bookings for one day stays.
First come, first served. Open all year.
Tel 015394 32733

Hostels
Elterwater Hostel (former Elterwater YHA, now private)
Tel 015394 37245
www.elterwaterhostel.co.uk

Great Langdale Bunkhouse (Stickle Barn)
NY 294 065 (next to New Dungeon Ghyll Hotel)
Friday and Saturday – 2 night bookings only
www.greatlangdalebunkhouse.co.uk
Tel 01539 437725

Stage 3/3A
Hotels, inns and B&Bs
The Scafell Hotel
Rosthwaite
Tel 017687 77208
http://scafell.co.uk

Royal Oak
Rosthwaite
Tel 017687 77214
www.royaloakhotel.co.uk

Hazel Bank Country House
Rosthwaite
Tel 017687 77248
www.hazelbankhotel.co.uk

Yew Tree Farm
Rosthwaite
Tel 017687 77675
http://borrowdaleyewtreefarm.co.uk

Borrowdale Gates Hotel
Grange
Tel 017687 77204
www.borrowdale-gates.com

The Keswick area has an enormous number of hotels and B&Bs.
Tourist Information Centre (also covering Borrowdale):
Tel 017687 75738
www.keswick.org

Campsites
Stonethwaite Farm
Stonethwaite
NY 268 133
Tel 017687 77234

YHA Borrowdale
Longthwaite
Rosthwaite
NY 255 142
Tel 0345 3719624
Open summer and selected weekends.
25 spaces for tents

APPENDIX C
Accommodation stage by stage

Stage 1
Hotels, inns and B&Bs
There are quite a few hotels and B&Bs in Ulverston.
For up-to-date information:
www.chooseulverston.co.uk
info@chooseulverston.co.uk

Torver, along with the hamlet of Little Arrow to the north, has a couple of B&Bs and a couple of pubs.

There are several hotels, inns and B&Bs in Coniston.
Tourist Information Centre:
Tel 015394 41533
www.conistontic.org

Wilson's Arms
Torver
Tel 015394 41237
www.thewilsonsarms.co.uk

The Old Rectory
Little Arrow
Torver
Tel 015394 41353
www.theoldrectoryhotel.com

The Church House Inn
Torver
Tel 015394 49159
www.thechurchhouseinn.com

Campsites
Priory View (Camping and Caravan club certified site)
Sandhall
Ulverston
SD 305 770
Tel 01229 586805

Scarr Head Camping Site
Torver
SD 283 947
Tel 015394 41576
Open Mar–Oct

Coniston Hall
Haws Bank (Lake District)
Coniston
SD 304 959
Tel 015394 41223
Open Mar–Oct

Hoathwaite campsite
SD 296 949
Torver
Tel 015394 32733
Open late Mar–Oct
No advance bookings for one-day stays

Youth Hostels
None at Ulverston

YHA
Coniston
Holly How
Tel 0345 371 9511
conistonhh@yha.org.uk

YHA Coniston Coppermines Valley
Coniston (off route)
Tel 0345 3719630
coppermines@yha.org.uk

Stage 2/2A
Hotels, inns and B&Bs
There is an ever-changing list of small B&Bs en route to Great Langdale.
Tourist Information Centre
Tel 0844 225 0544

Skiddaw summit looking south (Stage 4A)

Carlisle is at present restricted to Wednesdays and Saturdays.

Caldbeck to Carlisle: The limited 73 service around the Skiddaw/Blencathra massif to Caldbeck and onwards to Carlisle is at present restricted to Wednesdays and Saturdays. A train service runs from Dalston to Carlisle (and Ulverston – long round trip) and service 75 also links Dalston and Carlisle.

Selected taxi companies

Ulverston
Geoff's Taxis
Tel 01229 586666

IC Taxis
Tel 01229 582765

Ambleside (for Great Langdale and Coniston)
Ambleside Hilltop Taxis
Tel 07979 664472

Keswick (for Borrowdale)
Davies Taxis
Tel 01768 772676

Carlisle
A2B Taxis
Tel 01228 424468

Metro Taxis
Tel 01228 522088

Baggage transfer service

The Sherpa Van Project
Tel 0871 5200124
info@sherpavan.com
www.sherpavan.com

Lake District Baggage Transfer
Tel 01768 88279 or 07485 657548
www.lakedistrictbaggagetransfer.com

Walking holiday companies

There are also walking holiday companies who arrange self-guided holidays on the Cumbria Way. They select the accommodation and transfer the baggage for you. You just do the walking.

Contours Walking Holidays
www.contours.co.uk

Absolute Escapes
www.absoluteescapes.com

Wandering Aengus
www.wanderingaengustreks.com

Walkers Britain
www.walkersbritain.co.uk

Skiddaw House (Stage 4)

DOWNLOAD THE ROUTES IN GPX FORMAT

All the routes in this guide are available for download from:

www.cicerone.co.uk/1133/GPX

as standard format GPX files. You should be able to load them into most online GPX systems and mobile devices, whether GPS or smartphone. You may need to convert the file into your preferred format using a conversion programme such as gpsvisualizer.com or one of the many other such websites and programmes.

When you follow this link, you will be asked for your email address and where you purchased the guidebook, and have the option to subscribe to the Cicerone e-newsletter.

www.cicerone.co.uk

LISTING OF CICERONE GUIDES

BRITISH ISLES CHALLENGES, COLLECTIONS AND ACTIVITIES
Great Walks on the England Coast Path
Map and Compass
The Big Rounds
The Book of the Bivvy
The Book of the Bothy
The Mountains of England and Wales:
    Vol 1 Wales
    Vol 2 England
The National Trails
Walking the End to End Trail

SHORT WALKS SERIES
Short Walks Hadrian's Wall
Short Walks in the Lake District: Keswick, Borrowdale and Buttermere
Short Walks in the Lake District: Windermere Ambleside and Grasmere
Short Walks in the Lake District: Coniston and Langdale
Short Walks in Arnside and Silverdale
Short Walks in Nidderdale
Short Walks in Northumberland: Wooler, Rothbury, Alnwick and the coast
Short Walks on the Malvern Hills
Short Walks in Cornwall: Falmouth and the Lizard
Short Walks in Cornwall: Land's End and Penzance
Short Walks in the South Downs: Brighton, Eastbourne and Arundel
Short Walks in the Surrey Hills
Short Walks Winchester
Short Walks in Pembrokeshire: Tenby and the south
Short Walks on the Isle of Mull
Short Walks on the Orkney Islands

SCOTLAND
Ben Nevis and Glen Coe
Cycling in the Hebrides
Cycling the North Coast 500
Great Mountain Days in Scotland
Mountain Biking in Southern and Central Scotland
Mountain Biking in West and North West Scotland
Not the West Highland Way
Scotland
Scotland's Best Small Mountains
Scotland's Mountain Ridges
Scottish Wild Country Backpacking
Short Walks in Dumfries and Galloway
Skye's Cuillin Ridge Traverse
The Borders Abbeys Way
The Great Glen Way
The Great Glen Way Map Booklet
The Hebridean Way
The Hebrides
The Isle of Mull
The Isle of Skye
The Skye Trail
The Southern Upland Way
The West Highland Way
West Highland Way Map Booklet
Walking Ben Lawers, Rannoch and Atholl
Walking in the Cairngorms
Walking in the Pentland Hills
Walking in the Scottish Borders
Walking in the Southern Uplands
Walking in Torridon, Fisherfield, Fannichs and An Teallach
Walking Loch Lomond and the Trossachs
Walking on Arran
Walking on Harris and Lewis
Walking on Jura, Islay and Colonsay
Walking on Rum and the Small Isles
Walking on the Orkney and Shetland Isles
Walking on Uist and Barra
Walking the Cape Wrath Trail
Walking the Corbetts
    Vol 1 South of the Great Glen
    Vol 2 North of the Great Glen
Walking the Galloway Hills
Walking the John o' Groats Trail
Walking the Munros
    Vol 1 — Southern, Central and Western Highlands
    Vol 2 — Northern Highlands and the Cairngorms
Winter Climbs in the Cairngorms
Winter Climbs: Ben Nevis and Glen Coe

NORTHERN ENGLAND ROUTES
Cycling the Reivers Route
Cycling the Way of the Roses
Hadrian's Cycleway
Hadrian's Wall Path
Hadrian's Wall Path Map Booklet
Pennine Way Map Booklet
The Coast to Coast Cycle Route
The Coast to Coast Walk
The Coast to Coast Map Booklet
The Pennine Way
Walking the Dales Way
The Dales Way Map Booklet

LAKE DISTRICT
Bikepacking in the Lake District
Cycling in the Lake District
Great Mountain Days in the Lake District
Joss Naylor's Lakes, Meres and Waters of the Lake District
Lake District Winter Climbs
Lake District:
    High Level and Fell Walks
    Low Level and Lake Walks
Mountain Biking in the Lake District
Outdoor Adventures with Children — Lake District
Scrambles in the Lake District —
    North
    South
Trail and Fell Running in the Lake District
Walking The Cumbria Way
Walking the Lake District Fells —
    Borrowdale
    Buttermere
    Coniston
    Keswick
    Langdale
    Mardale and the Far East
    Patterdale
    Wasdale
Walking the Tour of the Lake District

NORTH—WEST ENGLAND AND THE ISLE OF MAN
Cycling the Pennine Bridleway
Isle of Man Coastal Path
The Lancashire Cycleway
The Lune Valley and Howgills
Walking in Cumbria's Eden Valley
Walking in Lancashire
Walking in the Forest of Bowland and Pendle
Walking on the Isle of Man
Walking on the West Pennine Moors
Walking the Ribble Way
Walks in Silverdale and Arnside

NORTH—EAST ENGLAND, YORKSHIRE DALES AND PENNINES
Cycling in the Yorkshire Dales
Great Mountain Days in the Pennines
Mountain Biking in the Yorkshire Dales
The Cleveland Way and the Yorkshire Wolds Way
The Cleveland Way Map Booklet
The North York Moors
Trail and Fell Running in the Yorkshire Dales
Walking in County Durham
Walking in Northumberland
Walking in the North Pennines
Walking in the Yorkshire Dales:
    North and East
    South and West
Walking St Cuthbert's Way
Walking St Oswald's Way and Northumberland Coast Path

DERBYSHIRE, PEAK DISTRICT AND MIDLANDS
Cycling in the Peak District
Dark Peak Walks
Scrambles in the Dark Peak
Walking in Derbyshire
Walking in the Peak District — White Peak East
Walking in the Peak District — White Peak West

WALES AND WELSH BORDERS
Cycle Touring in Wales
Cycling Lon Las Cymru
Great Mountain Days in Snowdonia
Hillwalking in Shropshire
Mountain Walking in Snowdonia
Offa's Dyke Path
Offa's Dyke Map Booklet
Scrambles in Snowdonia
Snowdonia: 30 Low-level and Easy Walks
— North
— South
The Cambrian Way
The Pembrokeshire Coast Path
Pembrokeshire Coast Path Map Booklet
The Snowdonia Way
The Wye Valley Walk
Walking Glyndwr's Way
Walking in Carmarthenshire
Walking in Pembrokeshire
Walking in the Brecon Beacons
Walking in the Forest of Dean
Walking in the Wye Valley
Walking on Gower
Walking the Severn Way
Walking the Shropshire Way
Walking the Wales Coast Path

SOUTHERN ENGLAND
20 Classic Sportive Rides in South East England
20 Classic Sportive Rides in South West England
Cycling in the Cotswolds
Mountain Biking on the North Downs
Mountain Biking on the South Downs
Suffolk Coast and Heath Walks
The Cotswold Way
The Cotswold Way Map Booklet
The Kennet and Avon Canal
The Lea Valley Walk
The North Downs Way
North Downs Way Map Booklet
The Peddars Way and Norfolk Coast Path
The Pilgrims' Way
The Ridgeway National Trail
The Ridgeway Map Booklet
The South Downs Way
The South Downs Way Map Booklet
The Thames Path
The Thames Path Map Booklet
The Two Moors Way
Two Moors Way Map Booklet
Walking Hampshire's Test Way
Walking in Cornwall
Walking in Essex
Walking in Kent
Walking in London
Walking in Norfolk
Walking in the Chilterns
Walking in the Cotswolds
Walking in the Isles of Scilly
Walking in the New Forest
Walking in the North Wessex Downs
Walking on Dartmoor
Walking on Guernsey
Walking on Jersey
Walking on the Isle of Wight
Walking the Dartmoor Way
Walking the Jurassic Coast
Walking the Sarsen Way
Walking the South West Coast Path
South West Coast Path Map Booklet
— Vol 1: Minehead to St Ives
— Vol 2: St Ives to Plymouth
— Vol 3: Plymouth to Poole
Walks in the South Downs National Park
Cycling Land's End to John o' Groats

ALPS CROSS—BORDER ROUTES
100 Hut Walks in the Alps
Alpine Ski Mountaineering Vol 1 — Western Alps
The Karnischer Hohenweg
The Tour of the Bernina
Trail Running — Chamonix and the Mont Blanc region
Trekking Chamonix to Zermatt
Trekking in the Alps
Trekking in the Silvretta and Ratikon Alps
Trekking Munich to Venice
Trekking the Tour du Mont Blanc
Tour du Mont Blanc Map Booklet
Walking in the Alps

FRANCE, BELGIUM, AND LUXEMBOURG
Camino de Santiago — Via Podiensis
Chamonix Mountain Adventures
Cycle Touring in France
Cycling London to Paris
Cycling the Canal de la Garonne
Cycling the Canal du Midi
Mont Blanc Walks
Mountain Adventures in the Maurienne
Short Treks on Corsica
The GR5 Trail
The GR5 Trail —
Vosges and Jura
Benelux and Lorraine
The Grand Traverse of the Massif Central
The Moselle Cycle Route
Trekking in the Vanoise
Trekking the Cathar Way
Trekking the GR10
Trekking the GR20 Corsica
Trekking the Robert Louis Stevenson Trail
Via Ferratas of the French Alps
Walking in Provence — East
Walking in Provence — West
Walking in the Auvergne
Walking in the Brianconnais
Walking in the Dordogne
Walking in the Haute Savoie: North
Walking in the Haute Savoie: South
Walking on Corsica
Walking the Brittany Coast Path
Walking in the Ardennes

PYRENEES AND FRANCE/SPAIN CROSS—BORDER ROUTES
Shorter Treks in the Pyrenees
The Pyrenean Haute Route
The Pyrenees
Trekking the Cami dels Bons Homes
Trekking the GR11 Trail
Walks and Climbs in the Pyrenees

SPAIN AND PORTUGAL
Camino de Santiago: Camino Frances
Costa Blanca Mountain Adventures
Cycling the Camino de Santiago
Mountain Walking in Mallorca
Mountain Walking in Southern Catalunya
Spain's Sendero Historico: The GR1
The Andalucian Coast to Coast Walk
The Camino del Norte and Camino Primitivo
The Camino Ingles and Ruta do Mar
The Mountains Around Nerja
The Sierras of Extremadura
Trekking in Mallorca
Trekking in the Canary Islands
Trekking the GR7 in Andalucia
Walking and Trekking in the Sierra Nevada
Walking in Andalucia
Walking in Catalunya —
Barcelona
Girona Pyrenees
Walking in the Picos de Europa
Walking La Via de la Plata and Camino Sanabres
Walking on Gran Canaria
Walking on La Gomera and El Hierro
Walking on La Palma
Walking on Lanzarote and Fuerteventura
Walking on Tenerife
Walking on the Costa Blanca
Walking the Camino dos Faros
Portugal's Rota Vicentina
The Camino Portugues
Walking in Portugal
Walking in the Algarve

Walking on Madeira
Walking on the Azores

SWITZERLAND
Switzerland's Jura Crest Trail
The Swiss Alps
Tour of the Jungfrau Region
Trekking the Swiss Via Alpina
Walking in Arolla and Zinal
Walking in the Bernese Oberland — Jungfrau region
Walking in the Engadine — Switzerland
Walking in the Valais
Walking in Ticino
Walking in Zermatt and Saas—Fee

GERMANY
Hiking and Cycling in the Black Forest
The Danube Cycleway Vol 1
The Rhine Cycle Route
The Westweg
Walking in the Bavarian Alps

POLAND, SLOVAKIA, ROMANIA, HUNGARY AND BULGARIA
The Danube Cycleway Vol 2
The High Tatras
The Mountains of Romania

SCANDINAVIA, ICELAND AND GREENLAND
Hiking in Norway — South
Trekking the Kungsleden
Trekking in Greenland — The Arctic Circle Trail
Walking and Trekking in Iceland

SLOVENIA, CROATIA, SERBIA, MONTENEGRO AND ALBANIA
Hiking Slovenia's Juliana Trail
Mountain Biking in Slovenia
The Islands of Croatia
The Julian Alps of Slovenia
The Mountains of Montenegro
The Peaks of the Balkans Trail
The Slovene Mountain Trail
Walking in Slovenia: The Karavanke
Walks and Treks in Croatia

ITALY
Alta Via 1 — Trekking in the Dolomites
Alta Via 2 — Trekking in the Dolomites
Day Walks in the Dolomites
Italy's Grande Traversata delle Alpi
Italy's Sibillini National Park
Ski Touring and Snowshoeing in the Dolomites
The Way of St Francis
Trekking Gran Paradiso: Alta Via 2
Trekking in the Apennines
Trekking the Giants' Trail: Alta Via 1 through the Italian Pennine Alps
Via Ferratas of the Italian Dolomites Vol 1
Vol 2
Walking in Abruzzo
Walking in Italy's Cinque Terre
Walking in Italy's Stelvio National Park
Walking in Sicily
Walking in the Aosta Valley
Walking in the Dolomites
Walking in Tuscany
Walking in Umbria
Walking Lake Como and Maggiore
Walking Lake Garda and Iseo
Walking on the Amalfi Coast
Walks and Treks in the Maritime Alps

IRELAND
The Wild Atlantic Way and Western Ireland
Walking the Kerry Way
Walking the Wicklow Way

EUROPEAN CYCLING
Cycling the Route des Grandes Alpes
Cycling the Ruta Via de la Plata
The Elbe Cycle Route
The River Loire Cycle Route
The River Rhone Cycle Route

INTERNATIONAL CHALLENGES, COLLECTIONS AND ACTIVITIES
Europe's High Points
Walking the Via Francigena Pilgrim Route —
Part 1
Part 2
Part 3

AUSTRIA
Innsbruck Mountain Adventures
Trekking Austria's Adlerweg
Trekking in Austria's Hohe Tauern
Trekking in Austria's Zillertal Alps
Trekking in the Stubai Alps
Walking in Austria
Walking in the Salzkammergut: the Austrian Lake District

MEDITERRANEAN
The High Mountains of Crete
Trekking in Greece
Walking and Trekking in Zagori
Walking and Trekking in Corfu
Walking on the Greek Islands — the Cyclades
Walking in Cyprus
Walking on Malta

HIMALAYA
8000 metres
Everest: A Trekker's Guide
Trekking in the Karakoram

NORTH AMERICA
Hiking and Cycling the California Missions Trail
The John Muir Trail
The Pacific Crest Trail

SOUTH AMERICA
Aconcagua and the Southern Andes
Hiking and Biking Peru's Inca Trails
Trekking in Torres del Paine

AFRICA
Kilimanjaro
Walking in the Drakensberg
Walks and Scrambles in the Moroccan Anti-Atlas

NEW ZEALAND AND AUSTRALIA
Hiking the Overland Track

CHINA, JAPAN, AND ASIA
Annapurna
Hiking and Trekking in the Japan Alps and Mount Fuji
Hiking in Hong Kong
Japan's Kumano Kodo Pilgrimage
Trekking in Bhutan
Trekking in Ladakh
Trekking in Tajikistan
Trekking in the Himalaya

TECHNIQUES
Fastpacking
The Mountain Hut Book

MINI GUIDES
Alpine Flowers
Navigation
Pocket First Aid and Wilderness Medicine
Snow

MOUNTAIN LITERATURE
A Walk in the Clouds
Abode of the Gods
Fifty Years of Adventure
The Pennine Way — the Path, the People, the Journey
Unjustifiable Risk?

For full information on all our guides, books and eBooks, visit our website:
www.cicerone.co.uk

CICERONE

Trust Cicerone to guide your next adventure, wherever it may be around the world...

Discover guides for hiking, mountain walking, backpacking, trekking, trail running, cycling and mountain biking, ski touring, climbing and scrambling in Britain, Europe and worldwide.

Connect with Cicerone online and find inspiration.

- buy books and ebooks
- articles, advice and trip reports
- GPX files and updates
- regular newsletter

cicerone.co.uk